Land Girls Gang Up

PAT PETERS

Old Pond Publishing

First published 2009

Copyright © Pat Peters, 2009
The moral right of the author has been asserted

ISBN 978-1-905523-95-5

A catalogue record for this book is available from the
British Library

Published by
Old Pond Publishing
Dencora Business Centre
36 White House Road
Ipswich
IP1 5LT
United Kingdom

Pri   ress

Contents

By this personal message I wish to express to you

Miss May Francis Davis.

my appreciation of your loyal and devoted service
as a member of the Women's Land Army from
8th. July 1943   to   11th. May 1946.

Your unsparing efforts at a time when the victory
of our cause depended on the utmost use of the
resources of our land have earned for you the
country's gratitude.

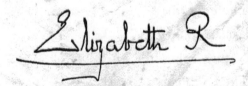

Preface

IT was a chance conversation with the author's son, Ashley, which led to my friendship with Pat. I was researching the lives of land girls in Cornwall for a book by a local publisher. Pat generously lent me her milking coat, breeches and dungarees for my work in schools and I became enthralled by the vivid memories of her time in the Land Army. Again, by chance, she told me she had written them down.

'Good enough for a series like *Dad's Army*,' she still maintains.

For her, despite a great deal of hard work, time on the land was full of laughter and joyful escapades.

Her memories tell of a group of young girls who were representative of those from all over England and from all walks of life, thrown together on farms in Cornwall to help feed a nation at war. Girls whose skills, friendships and memories are more important in today's world than ever before.

ANGIE BUTLER
Penzance, 2009

Chapter 1

The Initiation

I WOKE up without the usual constant calls from my mother telling me it was time to get up for work. It was a beautiful sunny day and my spirits rose when I looked at the uniform that lay on a chair beside my bed. It was the uniform of the WLA (Women's Land Army), and at last the day had come when I could wear it and call myself a member of the Armed Forces. Armed? I smiled as I glanced at the neatly packed kitbag propped up against the bedroom wall.

My equipment in the long khaki bag consisted of two pairs of working dungarees, three fawn shirts, a second thick green jumper, three pairs of long fawn socks, two milking coats, a heavy pair of leather boots, a pair of wellingtons, a strong thick fawn mackintosh and a sou'wester. On top of the clothes was an oblong tin box that held a flask. These were to carry lunch and tea to the fields wherever I was needed to work as a land girl.

Such was the 'armoury' with which I had been issued a week earlier in readiness for use during the months or years ahead . . . until the war was over. I had volunteered in June and had passed a strict medical before being accepted. Patiently and eagerly I had waited for the final official papers that would tell me where and when to go. Now, at last, my services were needed to fill a vacancy in Cornwall on 30th August, 1943.

My mother appeared in the doorway balancing a tray. She was smiling. 'Now it's your turn to leave, why not have breakfast in bed? Don't let those old farmers work you too hard and be careful if you get near cows and horses. Oh dear, I feel so scared just thinking about what you may have to do. Never mind, stand up for yourself and tell the farmers to milk their own cows.

'At least you'll be away from all this horrible bombing and black-outs. Perhaps the Germans don't know where Cornwall is and they won't want the Land Army anyway. As for the colour of your uniform, the green and brown will camouflage you in the fields. Green! Ugh!'

'Don't be superstitious, Mum, and stop worrying. It's going to be fun and I'm not afraid of cows – at least, I don't think I am! Now, I've got to get dressed.'

The laces just below the knees of the breeches caused some laughter. Tied too tight and I couldn't bend my knees; tied loosely and the long fawn socks bulged out in an unsightly fashion. Even when the laces were fastened comfortably and the socks pulled up, the flat brown shoes took away any remaining shreds of elegance.

The only item of the uniform that could be changed and made to look a little more becoming was the hat, which was made of brown felt and could be pushed into several different styles. I chose to wear mine tilted on the back of my head. When I put my greatcoat on I felt as if I had gained two stone in weight – but there was no time to stop and think about gravity. I had to catch a bus to Paddington station and there was yet the added load of my kitbag to contend with. Dragging it to the top of the stairs, my mother and I gave it a push and it rolled down the stairs and on to the front door.

'Well, your boots and wellingtons are at the door waiting to go, so I suppose you had better join them and be off!' Although my Mother had a lovely sense of humour I knew that she cared for each member of her family and I saw her expression change to apprehension as I opened the front door and swung my kitbag. It missed my left shoulder, fell to the ground and I found myself on top of it with the corner of the tin box sticking in my ribs. Just at that moment the postman appeared.

'I'm not going to help you up,' he laughed. 'In a month's time you'll be swinging the bull around – that's if he hasn't tossed you first.'

'All you've got is a little bag to carry and it's nearly always empty so you are not so smart.' I replied indignantly.

'I can't help it if the bloody Germans stop the love letters from our lads getting through. Be a good girl and see that you write home every day to your mother and she'll let me know if you've toughened up. Good luck and heave-ho!' He started to walk on and then retraced his steps to our front gate.

'Are you Miss M Davis by any chance?' he asked, holding a letter. 'Yes, I am. Is that a letter for me?'

'Only half a letter, I bet. The bloody Germans love playing with fire bombs. This one is from the Middle East and is scorched and I bet half the words inside are blue-pencilled. Still, at least he's alive so let him know you are too.' He went on his way whistling and I made a second successful attempt at shouldering my kitbag. Turning to my mother I knew that I was going to get the full treatment.

'Are you sure you have got your ration book? Have you got your identity card? How about your health card? Mind you don't lose your gas-mask. Let me come to the station with you, there might be an air-raid.'

'Stop fussing. If you come with me and there's an air-raid what will *you* do?' She hadn't thought about her own safety.

'I can take care of myself. You are only seventeen and if you miss the train they could have you up for desertion.' She said the last few words so seriously that I burst out laughing and dropped my kitbag again.

I looked down at my mother, a small woman who didn't stand higher than my shoulder. Two years earlier she had lost her eldest son and I, my brother, who had been a sergeant in the army. She had borne the loss with such courage once the tears had stopped flowing. Her second son had injured his leg and was in an army hospital. Her third son was in the RAF over in America training to be a pilot. My nineteen-year-old sister was in Coventry working in an ammunition factory, whilst my father was a chef in a similar factory in Staffordshire. The three youngest members of the family were safely evacuated to Devon, so I was the last link in her broken chain of a wartime family.

I kissed her goodbye and struggled to the nearby tram stop. Ten minutes later I had transferred from the tram to a bus that took me to Paddington – and utter confusion.

The station was no longer grey and dreary. Men and women dressed in airforce blue hurried by, intermingling with those wearing the army khaki. Sailors, Wrens and American soldiers all had a purpose and were heading towards a platform. Standing with my kitbag at my side I watched the chaos. Within seconds panic began to assail me. Although instructions had been sent to me from Middlesex regarding the station, the train departure and my destination, there had been no mention of platform number! My eyes sought and followed girls dressed in the brown and green uniform of the WLA. Many were arriving alone and looking bewildered while others came in groups, all heading in the same direction.

Following like a lost sheep I found myself on a platform amongst hundreds of new WLA recruits. Some girls were accompanied by a parent or parents who were either standing by proudly watching their particular offspring or were fussing about travel warrants etc. I was aware of the feelings of this second group – I had been through that! The train doors were not yet unlatched but I had been assured that this was the one and only train going to the west, right down to Penzance, the end of the railway line.

I remember the hubbub of shouts and laughter and the sun blazing down on us through the glass dome above the platform. The fact that there was a world war raging and this being the reason we were there seemed to elude both parents and girls. How many of these young (and some very attractive) females, I wondered, wore the unflattering uniform for patriotic reasons? How many, like myself, had volunteered to join the WLA simply because they loved the countryside and had romantic visions of milking a cow?

Whatever the motive that had drawn us together, here we were, waiting for the 10.30 am train to take us to various stops down in the West Country. At last, doors were opened and a voice loud and clear echoed from the station's loudspeaker, informing all and sundry not to be under any illusion that peace was secured simply because this large and boisterous contingent of the WLA had joined up!

Having disposed of our kitbags, which incidentally called for several attempted swings before they rested up on the luggage rack, we stood tentatively summing each other up, eight occupants in the compartment. With five minutes to go before Exodus, faces expressed the excitement of a long-awaited adventure. Indeed, many of the girls had never journeyed into the countryside, as they were to confess later. Clouds of steam belched from under the train, doors were slammed and whistles blew, but above all the din we could hear the farewell shouts of 'Don't forget to write!' coming from the parents. The order was echoed by the porters as they mopped their brows and sighed with relief!

I was fortunate to get a window seat, which let me give my attention to my companions sitting opposite and to my left, as well as see the fields as the train sped by. Conversation between us was immediate, with the inevitable 'What part of Cornwall are you going to?' and 'What part of London do you come from?' We shared and swapped sandwiches and offered the few sweets that we had. My mother, unknown to me, had put in a bar of chocolate taken from her own sweet ration. The red sign displaying NON SMOKER was ignored and the few cigarettes we were lucky to have were broken in half before we lit up.

Once again my mother had helped me. Before she cooked my breakfast she had gone out and queued at the local newspaper shop and had practically begged for an extra five cigarettes which were grudgingly handed to her in thin paper. She had given them to me with a look of triumph!

When we decided to smoke we formed a circle holding our halved cigarette and carefully passed the single match around. Not only was the match struck, a special comradeship sparked amongst us. We were Londoners, we were young and had left school at the age of fourteen to be faced with four years of blackouts, bombing and food and clothes rationing. Now we were off to a county many miles away from home and a completely new way of life, a life entirely different from factories and offices. Our spirits were high, our expectations were *fun*!

We were all getting on well when the carriage door swung open. A slim girl stood in the doorway busily rolling up the sleeves of her green jumper. In a loud voice she asked, 'Who wants a bleedin' fight?'

I cringed further into my corner seat and stared unseeingly out of the window, quite aware that this aggressive figure was looking from one to the other waiting for a response. An ominous silence fell over the carriage. Not getting any reaction from us the green and brown clad figure moved on down the corridor. Again, a door was pushed open and we heard the loud cockney voice repeating her request for a battle: 'Who wants a bleedin' fight?'

She sounded determined but it was evident that no

answer was forthcoming from that compartment either. A door slammed again and another loud demand for an opponent echoed down the corridor! Looking at the girls opposite I half smiled and they grinned back at me but I had the feeling that we were all frightened, at least a little. Who was she and why the unprovoked attack?

Relaxing, I pulled out my enrolment paper from my pocket and tried to memorize my given number, 130669. This was followed with instructions on where to catch the train and to disembark at Liskeard at 4.10 pm. A billet was being arranged, immediate employment was Gang Work and my employer was the Cornish War Agricultural Executive Committee; wage 45/0d per 48-hour week. There would be a 10 per cent abatement and the cost of the billet would be £1, so the sum total of pocket money would be 19/11d.

At Plymouth those of us who were heading for the far west scrambled out on to the platform and rushed to the buffet to buy some much-needed drinks, only to be faced with a long queue of soldiers. Undaunted, our potential aggressor, with her sleeves still rolled up and brimmed hat set firmly and correctly on her head, went into the buffet ahead of us and took complete charge. A few loud words telling them to make way for a real army and a clenched fist from her brought about a quick dispersal! To the accompaniment of a chorus of wolf whistles we bought our liquid refreshments and dived back into the locomotive, still wondering who *she* was.

Did she have some kind of authority over us or was she simply asserting her toughness?

Once over the Tamar bridge I leaned back with closed eyes for a few minutes thinking of how I had nearly joined the Wrens . . . assuming the Wrens would have let me join them! Why didn't I? The very thought of having to salute and adhere to rules and regulations was sufficient to make me rebel. Was I a person to refuse allegiance to sovereign or country? No, I wished to 'do my bit' with the maximum amount of freedom – and what better way to achieve this service other than in the fresh air with the WLA?

At last the train drew into Liskeard. Now I would see whom I was destined to work alongside during the next few months or even longer and perhaps get a first taste of things to come. After struggling to get my kitbag down from the luggage rack with no success I turned to the seven girls watching me with amusement.

'Would one of you please help me lift it down?' I asked.

'You're on your own now mate. Got to be tough in this orphanage so just help yourself,' said the dark-haired and generously bosomed girl who had sat on my left chewing gum for the entire journey. She went under the name of Peggy. With a final heave and groan from me, the long round bag fell with a thud across another girl's lap, knocking her hat from her head en route. I regarded the scene for only a few seconds before staggering out on to the platform murmuring my apologies as I turned and closed the door.

A little further down the platform a middle-aged man was pacing up and down waving his arms with great agitation. Panic was spread over his face and it soon became obvious that he was trying to delay the train that was about to leave. With the help of a guardsman he gathered nine bewildered girls together and spluttered, 'Get into the train agin, there's no work for 'ee 'ere, go on to Penzance.' We were pushed into yet another compartment, our kitbags thrown in behind us. One girl (I later knew to be Doris), had to stand all the way to the next station with the tail of her greatcoat held firmly in the door catch! Needless to say she was more than a little irritated and let out a torrent of language fit for any army barracks.

As we approached Marazion the coast came into view. About a mile out from the shore, surrounded by a lovely blue sea rose a fairytale sight: a mount with a turreted castle on the top. We could see a little row of houses at the bottom of the mount and tucked beside the small houses was a church. Trees grew up the steep sides of the mount. The train had slowed down and I stood gazing from the window at this romantic sight. Since leaving Plymouth we had sped through fields and seen odd-looking mine shafts but this sight was my first enchanting impression of Cornwall. The sun was still high in the sky and several little boats were tied to the island harbour. A guard came along the corridor telling us that we were nearing Penzance.

'What is that out in the sea?' I asked him.

'That's St Michael's Mount, miss. You'll see it often.'

'Who lives there?'

'Lord St Levan, he owns it. Wouldn't like it myself. Listen to the crowd of them!' He was referring to the girls who were singing about the advantages of being 'beside the seaside'. Voices were raised in song all the way to Penzance and on the station itself. So loud was it that people came rushing into the station, only to halt suddenly and stare.

After being counted and ticked off a list by a man called Mr Wilson who had come from Truro, we were promptly hustled into a lorry and driven to a hostel a mile out of Penzance. The singing became louder as we went along the road to Poltair hostel. The lorry halted outside this large building and we shuffled up the short drive. A big brown door opened and a matronly soul appeared.

There was a moment of charged silence and then the cockney voice rang out. 'Wotcha cock, we're here.' Laughter sprang from the forty or so girls, relieving the anti-climax of the end of the journey. A roll call and then we were shown to our respective dormitories, which were equipped with bunk beds. This was the point where I was to meet a lifelong friend. She had pretty blonde hair, brown eyes and a slim figure. We both stood by a bunk in the corner of the dormitory and decided to spin a coin for the bottom bunk. I lost the toss.

'I am Cathy but call me Kay,' she said with a smile.

'I was christened May and I don't like it.'

'You don't look like a May so why not be a Pat?'

As this was a favourite name of mine I had no hesitation in adopting this pseudonym. We didn't know it at the time, but this was the moment of several secular baptisms beside bunk beds! Lily became Jackie, Violet renamed herself Bunny and Jimmy conveniently forgot who she was! While we were in the middle of unpacking our kitbags and stacking our clothes in long tin cupboards there was a commotion at the other side of the dormitory. The cockney voice was again raised, this time in surprise and excitement as she watched Pauline who was unpacking beside her.

'What the bleedin' 'ell you got there?' she asked.

Pauline held up a satin slip, a pretty peach edged in coffee-coloured lace. 'You're nothing but a bleedin' snob! Fancy bringing stuff like that down here. Christ! You're in the bloody Land Army now.'

Pauline sat bewildered and frightened. 'But Nell . . .' she began. So! Our self-assured cockney was called Nell.

Taking a large box from Pauline's cupboard Nell demanded to be told what the contents were, so Pauline undid a wide ribbon and lifted the lid timidly. The box was full of small bars of chocolate of different flavours shaped like polar bears.

'Where the 'ell did you get these? You didn't nick 'em, did you?' All eyes were now on Pauline who was looking so embarrassed.

'No, Nell,' she stammered. 'My boyfriend sent them to me from Iceland. You have one – in fact, take half of them.'

'I don't want half of them. I'll take one and you can pass the rest around,' Nell ordered. Without hesitation, Pauline offered the box at every bunk. Nell, it seemed, was quite prepared to forgive Pauline for appearing to be a snob, and we were quite prepared to overlook Nell's aggression. She wasn't greedy, and as she said, 'We share this room so we share the good and bad.'

After a wash and a meal we crowded into the lounge. Kay went over to the piano and once again singing broke out, but not for long. Gradually we drifted back to our bunks to write those 'Don't forget to write' letters. When the lights were turned off there were more than one tear shed, including mine. The quietness of the country seemed uncanny. No sirens, no drone of aeroplanes, no screaming of falling bombs, no hissing of flying shrapnel. It was indeed all very peaceful down in the West, until the hoot of an owl was heard from a nearby tree. 'Hell's bells,' Jackie moaned to her pillow, 'I'm scared stiff!'

Chapter 2

On Holiday

To be awakened at 7 am was no shock. Many of us had risen much earlier than this when travelling to our previous jobs. Time had to be allowed for queuing for trams and buses. If there had been a heavy air-raid during the night it often meant walking the six or seven miles in darkness, dodging firemen and their hoses who had worked throughout the night, putting out the blazing fires caused by the German incendiary bombs. If it wasn't fires then it was demolished buildings that delayed us getting to work. Sometimes the obstruction was due to an unexploded time bomb and a long detour had to be taken away from the sealed-off area.

All these obstacles had been taken in one's stride, yet here in Cornwall and away from the enemy's harassment, moans came from a bunk bed across the other side of the dormitory and it wasn't long before we were all lamenting that we were already being punished by being awoken at this godforsaken hour. The matron had informed us that breakfast was at 8 o'clock and to be in the dining room on time. 'To arrive at 8.30 will be a joke on yourselves for you will find nothing to eat! And the next meal,' she added without a flicker of emotion, 'will not be until 12.30 pm so take your choice. Leave your bunks tidy, the bathrooms clean and all your belongings in the cupboards.'

As the matron turned to make her way to the floor above and a second dormitory, Nell shouted loudly and defiantly, 'Yes Sir! We'll do as you say but we ain't gonna salute you – ever!'

An hour later we were sitting round the three long dining tables when the door opened. Into the room glided Bunny. Her smile was radiant and revealed even white teeth and dimpled cheeks. All eyes were upon her as she walked slowly to a table, hovered, then passed to another table. She was, of course, looking for an empty seat. This girl was indeed the most glamorous of this unit. Her fair hair tumbled down in waves around her face to her shoulders. Did she stage this deliberate late entry? If so, it had the desired effect!

While we were finishing our breakfast and guessing among ourselves what the next move was to be, the door swung open again and in walked Mr Wilson with the matron on his heels. Looking more than a little perplexed he walked to the large window at the end of the room and stood with his back towards us for a few minutes before turning to face our enquiring looks. It was apparent that he felt humiliated for some reason.

'Girls,' he began, 'you have been enlisted a little too early. As yet there is no work for you, so for the time being you will have to amuse yourselves. Perhaps in a week's time someone will want you, so hang around and don't go further than Penzance. At all times wear your uniform and uphold the prestige of the Women's Land Army. I will come here again as soon as employment has been found.'

'Mate, unless we go out starkers we've got to wear our uniform!' There was no doubt now that Nell was going to be the first to retort with her sharp cockney humour. Yet at the same time, she was determined to see that we were not to be spoken to like fools. 'Hang around?' she continued, rising to her feet, 'I'm off right now. Come on, girls.'

The scraping of chairs caused such a commotion that the matron's voice went unheeded, the only words to reach our ears as we raced out of the dining room were '12.30 pm!' Not bothering to change from our working dungarees we touched up our make-up and filed out of the hostel congratulating ourselves on our cunning foresight in volunteering for the WLA.

As we neared the town a piercing scream came from Jackie who was in one of the first of the uneven groups jauntily swinging along.

'There's a bloody load of bulls let loose,' she cried in terror, before disappearing into a shop.

Nothing could have broken up the disjointed crocodile

walk faster than this warning! I stood transfixed with horror unable to respond to the sharp tugging on my arm from Kay who was at my side. Pauline came up from behind. 'For heavens sake, what's all the panic? The first few cows you see and an alarm is broadcast all over the vicinity that land girls are afraid. Look, here they come, there are only five and the farmer is behind them. Aren't they lovely?' Pauline stepped into the road to get a closer view as the animals passed, breaking into a trot when the farmer raised his voice.

'Dammit, miss, get back. Don't want any hindrance from you. Carry on to the market if you want to cuddle bullocks. Huh! Silly maid, you deserve to be kicked and stanked on.'

'What an awful man!' said Pauline feeling most indignant. From the direction of the town, dungaree-clad girls reappeared slowly like fugitives. Three girls stumbled from a telephone box, four ventured from a small florist's shop and about a dozen stepped cautiously from the West Cornwall hospital! Jackie joined us as we listened to an elderly man explaining that it was indeed market day and that there were lots more cattle further down the road. 'Cross this 'ere road now if you maids are scared but I tell 'ee, cows are frightened of 'ee.'

We took no chances and crossed the road. For months ahead all manifestations of bovine life were to be called bulls. Calves, yearlings, heifers, cows and steers – all from now on were to be given a wide berth!

As Kay and I approached the shops our thoughts turned to sending postcards home, for wasn't this a holiday? We did just that and having completed a tour of the shops were at a loss as what to do with ourselves next. Then a loud voice rang out.'Yoo hoo! . . . Yoo hoo!' The call came from Nell who was accompanied by Jackie. Both were sucking sticks of rock.

'If you ain't got nuffin to do come down to the prom wiv us, we might find some Yanks,' said Nell. Her tone conveyed that we were lifetime buddies and that the prime motive for being in the WLA was to 'find some Yanks'.

Laughing, we set off in what we thought was the direction of the sea. An easy enough feat one would have thought in this day and age, or any other, but back then we were never quite sure at what point of the compass the English Channel flowed – or was it the Atlantic Ocean that pounded the shores of Penzance? Totally ignorant of these geographical arrangements, in no time at all we were lost in the narrow back streets. Taking the initiative as always, Nell stopped the first male that came into view.

'Where's the prom, mate?' she asked.

The grey-haired man looked her up and down as if she had just descended from Mars.

'Do you mean the promenade, miss?' he countered. If he was lacking knowledge of abbreviations then I was similarly uninformed.

'Is there a difference then?' I asked innocently.

His blue eyes twinkled as he gazed at each of the four of us in turn and a smile spread over his face, a smile of comprehension.

'You be the land girls that came by train yesterday, oh yes!'

'Oh no,' Kay replied impishly, 'We arrived by plane last night.' Looking perplexed that he hadn't known this latest piece of gossip, he rubbed the lobe of his ear and frowned.

'Ah! I 'spect you flew into St Mawgan then, oh yes!'

'Oh no, we landed at Land's End,' Kay misinformed him.

'Ah yes, St Just,' he said knowingly, continuing to rub his lobe. 'Ah yes, a bomb dropped out there the other day and killed a cow. 'Tis some sad, you, some sad.'

'A cow? Sod your cows, mate,' said Jackie looking at the man disdainfully. Only too clearly she was remembering how frightened she had been a few hours ago when near the market. There was a sharp silence, it was obvious that cows meant as much to him as people did to us. Jackie went on contemptuously, 'In London people are getting killed and all you can sympathize with are bleedin' cows. You don't know there's a war on down here, mate.'

'Where did you say the promenade is?' I butted in.

28

'Go 'long the end of this 'ere road, turn left and it be just past the church.' He directed the way with an old gnarled stick, still wearing a puzzled look on his face. Thanking him, we turned, intrigued with the encounter made simply by losing ourselves. What was in store for us when confronted with more than one Cornishman? Would we hold our own as people or would we be slotted into the category of second-rate cows and be made to feel inferior to female oxen?

Following his instructions, we came in sight of the sea. On the beach there was evidence that the German army might have been expected to land in this part of England. Rolls of barbed wire lined the length of the shore; however, this seemed to be the only reminder that the country was at war on this sunny day. Apart from a couple of dozen land girls who had had the same idea as us, there were few people walking along the promenade, It was totally different from Southend pier and the south-east resorts that some of us had visited.

Joining the other girls sitting in the bandstand we discussed the merits of visiting the one and only dance hall in town, the Winter Gardens, which was sited on the promenade. Deciding it was worth a visit we returned to Poltair hostel. It was slow going, for the return journey was uphill all the way and there were no buses running.

When we went into the hostel the stern look on the matron's face told us it was well past 12.30. We had lost all sense of time! Trying to ignore her severe expression we proceeded to file into the dining room. As Kay and I neared the door she stepped deliberately in front of us barring our way. Behind Kay and me were Pauline, Nell and Jackie.

'Not so fast! The majority of the girls appear to have settled here already and are quite prepared to fall in with my orders, but as usual I see there are the few trouble-makers.' Her eyes scanned us as she went on. 'Have you no dignity along with no sense of time? The trades-men have been this morning and from their accounts there was chaos near the market shortly after you left. This is a quiet and peaceful town so see that it stays that way.'

'Tell the farmers to move their market, or move us!' said Jackie.

'We were not issued with watches, mate, and the town clock has stopped,' Nell added, 'and even if there were sundials around we couldn't read them. Christ! What's the fuss about?' For a second the matron and Nell eyed each other with hostility.

'I can see that you are determined to battle against authority and can only hope for your sake – and the sake of your little band of followers here – that you realize I can get you shifted immediately to a place where you will be on your own apart from cows and farmer!'

We opened our mouths and closed them again quickly. Here at this hostel at least we were assured of a few work-free days! The meal we were finally allowed to sit down to was almost cold but we didn't care. Rushing the food down, we hastened to the bathrooms and queued to wash our hair, then lay on the large lawn in the sun for the rest of the afternoon. Looking up at the clear blue sky I was vaguely aware of something missing. It was the absence of anti-aircraft barriers, barrage balloons! I sat up and glanced at the tall trees that surrounded the lawn. In less than two days, along with these other girls, I had been transported from town to country, from factory and friends to strangers and was glad to be here – and so near to the sea, too!

A gong resonated from inside the hostel summoning us for tea; none would be late for this meal! Once again Bunny came in last and she differed from the rest of us. While we sat with curlers in our hair, she took her place looking meticulous with make-up on and curlerless; she wasn't going to be seen ungroomed no matter what the cost. In fact she had stayed in her dormitory all afternoon, alone!

Not one of us had brought 'civvies'. Nothing in the call-up papers had suggested doing so, yet there was nothing suggesting not doing it either. Had one and all thought it would have been against any regulations? The idea hadn't crossed my mind, and even if it had there would have been no room for extra clothes. However, this was of little concern, the real anxiety we felt was due to the heavy brown shoes. Could we dance in them? Dressing beside our bunk I watched Kay alternately pulling up and pushing down the laced knees of her breeches, swearing in the process.

'What's the matter, Kay?' I asked. 'Why the agitation?'

'This is the second pair of breeches that don't fit properly!'

'Lucky you to be issued with two pairs. Was it a mistake?'

'No, the first pair that came were far too big, so last week I put them on with the rest of my uniform. I tied the waist with thick string to stop them falling down and went to Uxbridge to get them changed.' She sat on her bunk laughing as she told the story. 'On the way there I stopped for a cup of tea and spilt the lot over my breeches, so I looked a right sight when I arrived at the headquarters in Uxbridge. Not only were the breeches soaking wet, they were hanging almost to my ankles, dragging the socks down too!

'I had to face Gwenyth Jackson [the secretary] in this state. When I told her I wasn't going to travel to Cornwall looking like a tramp she hit the roof! "How dare you wear the uniform of one of Her Majesty's Services before officially becoming a member? That authorized date is the 30th of August. And look at your hat, you have practically ruined it. Cord under chin like a cowboy? How dare you!" She pulled my hat off, took the cords from each side and banged it into its original shape, then pushed it dead straight on my head. "In future see that you dress like a respectable land girl and not a person acting in a second-rate American picture. Your breeches will be changed but I forbid you to wear them until the day you get on the train." You can imagine how fast I left that building and I was too afraid to answer back.'

I certainly could imagine it, for I had donned my uniform as soon as it had arrived and circled the local park exhibiting myself with a friend. I had had my photograph taken, knowing that my action was contrary to military laws!

'Christ! I'm wearing my hat the way I want to,' said Jackie who had been listening, 'We're only in the Land Army, we ain't fighting so who cares? Lend us a fag before we go out.' Jackie wasn't so bold as to walk out of the hostel ahead of us on the second departure for the promenade, therefore the same five late girls were the last to leave and caught the lash of the matron's tongue as she issued another warning. 'Do not run amok in the hospital and people's houses tonight and I don't want to hear about any rumpus. Curfew is 11 o'clock.'

When we handed our greatcoats to the attendant at the Winter Gardens, Nell warned us in her customary loud voice, 'If anyone gets into trouble just shout for help and I'll come and sort them out! I'll be able to spot you quick in uniform.'

'And who you gonna sort out, honey? I hope it's gonna be me!' The drawling voice came from one of a bunch of Americans who were clearly amused at this slip of a girl playing protector.

'Wotch it, mate, these are my pals.' Nell looked the tallest and biggest American squarely in the face, quite undeterred. She had so far assumed roles of aggressor, spokesman, leader, and now she was our chaperone! Was she really so tough?

'Yanks!' Jackie beamed. 'Wot a bit of luck, I've just smoked me last fag. Let's get into the dance hall quick!'

Five young musicians formed the band and began to play a quickstep. We ignored the formal step and broke into the jitterbug, well aware of stony stares from the local girls standing on the edge of the dance hall. The band continued to play 'In The Mood' and soon the civilians were in a different frame of mind, the floor beginning to fill with bodies twisting and turning, though the reservation between WLA and civilians remained. Had their first impression of Nell scared them?

All too soon we had to leave, for it was a long and arduous trek back to the hostel. Before drifting out in twos and threes we arranged to meet outside Poltair and enter together. If one was to be late, far better we were all late!

A whispered roll call among ourselves revealed two missing. We'd wait a few minutes longer . . . then a further five minutes. No sign of them. It was established that the errant two were from the ground-floor dormitory so it was easy to form a plan and carry it out. Refusing the nightly drink of cocoa we went straight to the bunks of the missing girls and quickly pushed clothes in between the bunk sheets. We unlatched the large wooden shutters, opened the bottom window and pulled the shutters to again. Then we kept a sharp ear open for footsteps outside. This strategy was to be carried out many times during our short stay at the hostel; not once were we caught!

Four weeks passed and still no work was found. We spent the days walking through the countryside and along the coast to Newlyn and Mousehole. At Newlyn we struck up conversations with the local fishermen and at Mousehole we wandered through the narrow roads amazed at some of the tiny cottages. From these two villages St Michael's Mount could be seen clearly, in fact it dominated the bays for miles. Another focal point was the Lizard that could be seen on clear days.

In the evenings when we weren't dancing, we took many walks along the promenade. On a moonlit night little boats could be seen bobbing up and down on the sea. More than one conjured up visions of secret spies landing, even an odd German stormtrooper or two – but these stretches of our imagination were shattered when we were told that the little boats only held fishermen.

We were forever moaning about being woken up so

early, especially as there was no work to do, so we changed our routine. When we woke we would lie in bed for another half-hour then quickly dress and dash to the dining hall. After eating breakfast we back-tracked to the bathroom to undress and wash!

One afternoon towards the end of September as we were pottering in our dormitories, Mr Wilson appeared in a hurry and a lorry stood outside the hostel.

'I want twenty girls to come with me.' Picking at random he chose ten girls from the lower dormitory and ten from the upper. He disregarded any protests of 'I'm washing my hair' or 'I'm in the middle of writing a letter.' Fortunately he did listen to our pleas of keeping friends together, so Kay and I went along with Pauline and Phyllis, and Nell and Jackie joined us. From down the wide staircase Bunny came smiling, trying to look elegant with her kitbag. 'I'm going with you,' she said.

'Ain't no honour and nothing to smile about. It means work from now on, mate, and no dolling up, so don't look so bleedin' happy,' Nell told Bunny scathingly. With this she rounded on Mr Wilson, interrupting his third try to count the twenty girls he needed. 'By the way, where the 'ell are we going?' she demanded.

'To Wadebridge. It's about thirty miles away, so hurry. You will not be in a hostel. Private billets have been found for you and you will work for the Cornish Agricultural Committee. Tomorrow you'll find yourselves up on Tintagel moors picking potatoes. Come

36

on, we have a long way to go and tea will be waiting for
you.'

We scrambled up into the lorry. Odd bits of straw lay
on the floor and it stank like Penzance market.

'Hey you!' Nell rapped on the cab window to the
driver, 'come and clean this lorry out, we ain't a herd of
cows!'

The young driver gave Nell a wink, smiled and
started whistling while Mr Wilson secured the tail-end
of the truck. The engine started and we roared through
the streets of Penzance, our holiday over.

We were to learn later that this lorry was to be our
means of transport to and from various places of work,
and it was also to be a haven from the Cornish mists and
sometimes continual rain!

Chapter 3

Potatoes at Tintagel

THE journey to Wadebridge gave us the chance to get to know the names of the girls who had joined us from the top floor of the hostel. Apart from Bunny they had been only another lot of faces but now we were a gang of twenty, a gang to be working closely alongside each other.

The lorry pulled up outside Egloshayle church and Mr Wilson called for four girls to get out. Without any hesitation Nell jumped down, pulling her kitbag behind her and ordering Jackie to follow suit. They were shown into a small cottage. When two more were shouted for, Sue and Ann departed and vanished into a house near a river. The lorry moved slowly on down Egloshayle road before halting outside a row of pretty houses.

'One for here,' said Mr Wilson as he opened a gate, 'and two for next door, so hurry and make up your minds.'

'Let's go, Kay.' I said, quickly scrambling from the

lorry before anyone else took the chance. A low granite wall was topped with white railings and the small front garden was filled with flowers. Roses were growing each side of a bay window and at the end of the short garden path a coloured glass door was set under a white-painted porch. As the lorry drew away Pauline called to us: 'Phyllis and I are next so we won't be far away. See you at seven-thirty.'

Before the first two girls were dropped off we had arranged that we all meet by the Post Office at this given time. There could be only one such building in this small town, no one could possibly get lost!

I watched the small stocky form of Peggy disappear into the house next door. She was the dark-haired new recruit who had sat beside me chewing gum through the whole journey from Paddington to Penzance and still her jaws were working on the gum!

Kay and I were shown into our new billet by a dear old lady, Mrs Gill, and signed ourselves in as Catherine and May. However, after being taken to our shared attic bedroom we announced ourselves as Kay and Pat, completely confusing our landlady. 'Which is Cathy and which is Pat? Oh no, my dear life, it is Kay and May, am I right?' Corrected, she got flustered and ran down the stairs calling for Louis.

When we went down for tea we found that Louis was her husband. He took one look at us, grunted and carried on reading his newspaper. While eating tea we gave Mrs Gill an account of the bombing in London, the past month at the hostel and finally convinced her that we were known as Kay and Pat. The only recognition we got from Mr Gill were a few disgruntled 'Mmms' and meaningful stares.

At 7.30 the gang met and we reported to each other that 'lace curtains moved as we passed houses but not a soul was seen!' This was evidence that the inhabitants of Wadebridge knew of our arrival and were summing us up discreetly in their own homes. Jackie was the first to give her impression of Wadebridge: 'Gawd, what a place, there ain't no Yanks here,' she moaned. Nell agreed with her; these two girls were real cockneys and they would provide so much fun and laughter in future days.

The evening was still light and warm so we decided to look around the town. We walked to the long bridge that spanned the river Camel, a fifteenth-century structure with seventeen old pointed arches beneath and segmented arches on either side. (We were to learn a lot more about this bridge one rainy day.) We walked through the town and along the river, conscious all the time of being watched by unseen eyes, and bemoaning the fact that we were the only 'Forces' there.

As it grew dark we hastened to our billet, for like everywhere, there were blackout restrictions and we could no longer walk home in a crowd. Seven of the gang were housed along Egloshayle road, which ran from the eastern end of the bridge, four somewhere near the church, while the remaining nine girls were billeted not far from the railway station, the cinema and shops.

Bunny and Grace departed with a quiet 'Goodnight,' as they went up the steps to their lodgings. We had taken only a few steps when Nell shouted through the still night air: 'Don't forget to be at the church at eight tomorrow morning and cover up your 'air. Don't bother with your make-up, mate!'

Suddenly, lights in the row of houses went out and this time we saw curtains pulled aside – but still no faces were visible!

The following morning the lorry arrived shortly after 8 o'clock having already picked up the other nine girls from the bridge end. The driver, Roy, eyed us curiously from under his cap while an elderly man wearing an old fawn raincoat was introduced as our foreman, Cecil.

Barely had we settled in the lorry with our macs and tin food boxes on our laps when there was a screech of tyres and we were off to Tintagel, followed by a little man driving a little car who had a little dog sitting beside him. The man was our boss, Mr Knowles. He had uttered just four words: 'Off to Tintagel now.'

It was to be over half an hour's perilous ride. We clutched each other's arms tightly as the lorry swerved around the narrow roads, we half sprawled across each other when the lorry made a sudden halt and reversed to allow another vehicle to pass in a narrow lane. While we slithered and bumped in the back our eyes followed our tin boxes as they slid to and fro on the floor hitting our wellington-clad legs.

'He's a bloody maniac,' breathed Jackie before the lorry came to another sudden halt, throwing a dozen girls into a heap. Roy came to the back and started unpinning the chains that held the tail end in place, amusement spread all over his face. He winked at Cecil, who remained looking stony.

'Who do you bloody well think you are and what the 'ell do you think we are? Cows? I'll tell you now, mate,' Nell edged nearer to Roy, 'you ain't gonna give us a ride like that again, ever!'

Roy stood by, whistling, as he watched us jump from the lorry and rub our numb buttocks. We were led into a field where we were confronted by rows and rows of green leaves. Cecil explained that the leaves were the tops of 'teddies', the Cornish word for potatoes, and that we were here to pick them up. The sea lay to the right of this field and ahead in the distance was a row of hills.

'What are they called?' I asked Cecil, 'and in what direction are they?' There was so much to learn about this county of Cornwall and I realized how totally ignorant I was.

'They hills be called Brown Willy,' Cecil told me, making sure that the other girls also benefited from his knowledge. 'If you can see them hills it'll be a fine day, if they be covered in mist then we be in for mist and rain.'

Little Mr Knowles had been hovering near and spoke at last: 'Time you started work. Follow me.'

He led the way to the top of the field where a tractor stood beside a heap of sacks. On the tractor sat the driver with the inevitable cap upon his head, a ragged fawn raincoat held together with a piece of string hiding his other clothes.

'This is Jimmy Coombes. Now take a bundle 'tween two of 'ee and get in pairs.' Cecil ordered. He then proceeded to pace out even lengths of ground, stopping two girls at the end of each measurement of land and telling us that the bundles were 'markers'. Roy dropped two buckets near the markers and the tractor drove slowly down the furrows churning the potatoes above the earth.

'They are dirty and we have no gloves,' cried Bunny in dismay.

Cecil turned to her with a look of amusement, sucking in air between tongue and teeth. 'What the 'ell do 'ee want, the teddies washed for 'ee?' he asked, 'Get your back down and you won't be thinking about your 'ands.'

Waiting for Cecil, Roy and Mr Knowles to come together, Bunny asked sweetly, 'Where is the toilet, please?'

'There baint one out here,' Cecil answered, turning away.

'Wot! No bleedin' toilet?' Nell shouted in amazement, 'Where the bloody hell do we go, then?'

This last question left the three men with a dilemma. Three hands went up to lift three caps off to scratch three heads. A mumbled voice said something about 'the hedge'. This brought us to the stark realization that we would have to rough it!

At last our backs were bent and we faced newly dug potatoes which we put in buckets and then transferred to sacks. It wasn't long, however, before someone thought of moving the markers to their own advantage thus allowing them to finish their piece faster, turn their buckets upside down and rest upon them. This shortening of lengths was soon detected by the next couple, so they in turn moved their markers a few paces in their own favour. This plan of action went on right down the row until the two girls at the end were holding up the tractor and working much harder. A couple more rows were dug before they discovered what we had done.

'Hey!' shouted Sue who was working alongside Ann. 'We've got a longer piece than the others. Measure it out again or we stop work.'

Cecil looked around for Mr Knowles to help him with this dispute but the little man had vanished out of sight. Annoyed, Cecil sucked breath in between his teeth as before, while trying to visualize the measurements. 'Baint no good, I'll pace them out again. This sort of finagling usually starts at the end of rows.' He walked to the end where Jimmy and Peggy sat innocently on their buckets smoking a cigarette.

'Don't you blame them,' Nell warned Cecil, 'we're all guilty.'

'No mind, no mind. I'll sort it out later, it be crib time.'

'What time?' we asked, puzzled. Crib! A cot? Cards?

'Time to stop for a quick drink and something to eat,' Roy translated. He had alternately been walking up and down the furrows and standing by the lorry watching us, whistling all the time. We plodded over to the lorry and reached for our tin boxes, on which we had scratched our initials to avoid confusion.

'We can't eat with dirty hands,' Bunny announced with disgust. 'Isn't there a river nearby where we can wash?'

I smiled. Here we were, in the middle of nowhere, dirty and windswept, hungry and thirsty and yet the most important thing in her mind was that we wash before dining! Spitting saliva onto our hands, we got the worst of the mud off and ignored the dirt underneath our fingernails, letting out a series of 'Ughs!'

Taking a half-moon shaped object from her food box Nell exclaimed, 'I've got a bleedin' piece of pie crust!'

'Don't be a chump, it's a pasty and it's filled with

something,' Pauline told her, her eyes filled with laughter.

Jackie eyed her half-moon with suspicion before breaking it in half. Jam spilled from her pasty on to the knees of her dungarees. 'God, how I hate jam, and my sandwiches are cheese. God, how I hate cheese.'

Those who had pasties were to find that 'something' was to be almost anything. Kay and I found ours filled with potatoes, meat and onions while Pauline's and Phyllis's held egg and bacon. Bunny's had apples and Jimmy waved her pasty aloft proclaiming, 'Currants!'

The contents of our tin boxes, in future, were always to be a journey of discovery to some while others moaned about a monotonous supply of either cheese or fish-paste sandwiches.

Nearly half an hour passed and then Cecil began to look for his watch. To locate this timepiece was a task in itself. He loosened a length of string from around his waist, after which his hand pushed aside first a mac, then a waistcoat. Finally, the hand delved into a pocket and produced a small tin box. The lid of the box was raised and cotton wool lifted before the watch came into view. Fascinated, we watched as Cecil reversed his actions and more than one noted this operation and made a mental note to ask the time more often. It would give at least another five minutes respite from work!

'All right, girls, back to work. Roy has to go to Bodmin station at one o'clock with the potatoes.'

'Sod Roy, sod the potatoes,' Jackie muttered. 'I'm finishing my fag first and I'm going over to the hedge before I start again.'

This last statement made us aware that more time could be wasted if we walked to the farthest hedge! A whispered campaign resulted in the determined resolution that we would go back to work, wait for Jackie and Nell to reappear from the hedge then two more girls would disappear and so on. The relay took the gang nearly an hour to complete, leaving Cecil and Roy to fill in the empty spaces!

Mr Knowles had quickly disappeared when Bunny inquired about a toilet. The appearance of his little dog was a warning to all that he was about to come on the scene again and to keep our backs down. He said only a few words to Cecil and walked out of sight again prodding the earth with his walking stick to reveal potatoes left behind in the rows.

Waiting for the magic words telling us it was time for lunch, we were rather alarmed when Roy yelled one word from the lorry.

'Crouch!'

Looking around uncertainly we lowered ourselves and were almost lying flat when Cecil burst out laughing, enjoying a secret joke.

'He said croust, not crouch! What you afear'd of, the Germans?' Continuing to smile, Cecil had to explain the local dialect and we hurried to the lorry for the lunch break. Roy offered his penknife to Bunny, 'To clean your nails, me 'ansome,' he said. Roy slowly munched his sandwiches and stared adoringly at Bunny. He was only half-conscious of the other two men when they spoke to him.

'Roy, are you married?' The direct question came from Nell, causing the young, fair-haired driver to lower his eyes.

'Iss, 'ee be married sure 'nough,' Jimmy Coombes answered Nell's query. ''Ard luck if you're interested, miss.'

Nell glared at the tractor driver. 'You ain't funny, mate. As for you,' she turned to Roy, 'these girls are decent, so watch it. Keep your eyes and your hands on your steering wheel and there won't be any trouble over you!'

Roy, his face scarlet, left the lorry and looked towards the sea and then in the direction of Brown Willy.

'Dark clouds forming, Cecil. It's ragging for rain,' he said.

'Baint looking too good,' the foreman agreed with a frown.

'What happens if it rains?' asked Kay.

'If it baint too bad we carry on 'tween showers. If it skeats we sit in the lorry.' Bunny stood up, renewed her lipstick and combed her hair.

'Baint time to leave work yet, maid. So far you've done nort but traipse around the field trying to dodge work,' Cecil told her as he went through the ritual of uncovering his watch. He made his way back to the furrows with twenty girls dragging their feet behind him.

'We can pray for rain,' suggested Bunny.

'Who the 'ell do we pray to – Brown Willy?' grumbled Nell.

While we continued to pick up potatoes, Roy loaded the filled sacks and went off to Bodmin station complaining that it wasn't worth the journey with only forty-seven sacks!

As the afternoon wore on, our backs became increasingly painful. Each of us directed our moans at Cecil who began to show signs of sympathy until Jackie made her way to the hedge for the third time in two hours. He lost his temper and got down on one knee. 'You lot think you'm the boss but I tell 'ee you've 'ad it easy today. Tomorrow you'll do twice as much.'

Ignoring Cecil's forecast Jackie tapped her pocket to make sure her cigarettes were safe. 'Come on, Nell, bring your matches.' The relay was on again and the rests took longer behind the barrier of stone!

Dark clouds gathered above us, the sea had turned to an inky blue and Brown Willy couldn't be seen. Feeling cold, tired and hungry we began to pray that it *wouldn't* rain until Roy returned.

The lorry came in sight and Cecil relented. Gathering up odd sacks and putting a large boulder on them, he told us to make for the vehicle. 'You'll be feeling better tomorrow,' he added.

The journey back to Wadebridge was almost silent, a very subdued gang of girls sitting oblivious to how they looked. We even suffered in silence the erratic driving of Roy. Reaching our bedroom, Kay and I fell on the bed wondering why we had volunteered to help the war effort by working on the land. Without even washing we promptly fell asleep.

Chapter 4

The Cornish Arms

'CATHY and Pat – I mean Cathy and May – it be gone time to get up, me dears.' This came from Mrs Gill outside the bedroom door the following morning. She had not disturbed us for two hours after we had flopped on the bed the previous evening and we had only budged then to have a wash and a meal before collapsing on the bed again!

'Ouch! My back,' I muttered with eyes still shut.

Kay groaned too. 'Let's not go to work today,' she suggested. The temptation was almost irresistible. The sunshine streaming through the attic window was the only inducement to drag ourselves from the bed. We struggled down to the bathroom, repeatedly asking ourselves why we had been so reckless as to join the WLA. Why did we ache so badly? Half-bent, we splashed water over our faces and were dismayed to see our hair in a dirty, tangled mess. The coastal wind and dust from the potato field had played their parts well. Never had our hair looked so unclean and untidy. Wrapping our heads in scarves, turban fashion, we glanced at our dirty, engrained hands and shuddered. Just one day on the land and we both looked and felt like tramps! I thought of Bunny, how was she feeling?

With mackintoshes over our arms and carrying food boxes, we slouched to the church and sat on the wall with the other seven girls from the Egloshayle end of town and waited for the lorry, which arrived twenty minutes late. Slowly we clambered up to join some very dejected looking girls who were scowling at an old man who sat huddled in a corner amidst a cloud of pipe smoke.

'Who the 'ell are you and what are you smoking? Horse-dung?' Nell asked the newcomer who visibly squirmed at her question.

'I'm Mr Hornbrook. I be living for a while with my son Reg, same as Pauline and Phyllis. Are you the leader of this 'ere gang?'

'No one's leader and no one's Mr if they work with us, and you can put out that stinkin' thing you're puffin' for a start.'

'Me first pipe of the day. Dammit, don't none of 'ee smoke?'

'Smoke!' cried Jackie banging on the cab window. 'Can you stop at the nearest shop, Roy? I want to buy some fags.'

It was apparent that Cecil was exasperated at this late start.

'Dammit girls, we're late enough. Roy will have to drive like a bat out of hell as it is and that won't please 'ee.'

'Don't care, I want to buy some fags.' repeated Jackie.

'All right, perhaps we'll find a shop open at Camelford,' Roy called back impatiently and drove the lorry sharply away. We swayed against each other but didn't dare comment until Jackie had her cigarettes!

Passing through several small villages we suddenly came to a halt and several girls went sprawling with Nell underneath them. Mr Hornbrook smiled with delight and hugged his knees. 'You 'aven't felt full taste of 'is driving yet, maids. Many an accident 'e 'as 'ad, I can tell 'ee,' he chuckled.

'Christ! Can't the bugger drive?' Nell gasped. 'He'll kill us before any German gets the chance!'

'You want cigarettes? Here's a shop,' Roy shouted, unconcerned. Cecil came to the back of the lorry looking anxious, Roy sat whistling while the cause of the fracas crossed the road and disappeared into a shop.

On reaching Tintagel the second day, all eyes looked to the distance of Brown Willy. The hills were covered in mist and while we sent up a silent prayer that the wind would blow it all our way, Roy disappeared with the lorry and left us wondering what would happen if it rained.

'Don't worry,' Cecil said, 'it won't reach us till afternoon.'

Slowly and laboriously we worked the morning away with only screams from Jackie livening the boring task. As the tractor churned up row after row of potatoes large sea gulls dived swiftly towards us screeching and flapping their wings. One landed on a sackful of potatoes that stood only inches from Jackie as she was bent double. Forgetting the gnawing pain in her back she quickly straightened herself and ran to Cecil.

'Cecil, oh Cecil, do something. That bloody vulture is after me,' she cried. 'He's got his beak open screaming at me.'

'You be screeching louder than 'ee. Timmersome of a bird!' I turned and saw Mr Hornbrook sitting on a bundle of sacks hugging his knees again. 'Gesson do,' he carried on, 'they only be gulls and like as not I 'spect a brave few of 'em 'ave come all the way from St Ives to pick up your dog-ends, hee! hee!'

'Perhaps sniggering at us makes your day,' I said, 'and perhaps they are going to retrieve all the matches you have thrown away in order to help the war effort. It's called Save as you Slave.'

'Save? We don't save nort down this part of the world, maid.'

'Then I suggest you start right now and save your breath.' As I spoke the words I joined Kay and bent down. I knew that Nell was watching the old man closely and would have her say.

'Aren't you afraid of anything?' she asked him.

'I'm not 'urried about nort,' he laughed, and walked towards the end of the furrow not realizing that Nell was only silent because she hasn't understood his Cornish dialect!

The lorry came back just before noon. We sat in it eating our sandwiches and pasties while the four men happily sat sprawled on the earth with their food. We listened to their conversation and were both fascinated and amused. Apparently a sharp intake of breath against the bottom lip and the word 'iss' both meant the same . . . 'Yes!'

When Roy had finished eating he stood up in his dark blue overalls and suddenly burst into song. His tenor voice rang out:

> 'Old Mother Slipper Slopper jumped out of her bed,
> And out of the window she popped her head,
> Crying, John John John, the grey goose has gone,
> And the fox is off to his den-o, den-o, den-o.'

'Oh my God, his songs are as good as his driving,' said Kay, but Bunny asked him to sing a second verse. Roy beamed at her: 'Old Mother Slipper Slopper . . .'

While he sang about the fox going off to his den-o, we scrambled off to the hedge!

During the afternoon fatigue set in and we constantly glanced towards Brown Willy. The hills couldn't be seen. If this was a sign of bad weather, then why was it taking so long to reach us? Dark clouds had formed above and it became colder. Pauline reached for her mac and squealed with delight as she bent to the ground. The tractor was close behind her but was forced to stop as she continued to kneel and peer between some leaves. Jimmy Coombe left the tractor to inspect her find and, along with four girls nearby, I followed.

'Aren't they sweet?' Pauline held two tiny pink bodies in her cupped hands. A tinge of fine grey hair could be seen growing from the pink skin and little tails protruded from one end.

'What the 'ell are they?' asked Jackie backing away.

'Vermut! Scat 'em!' shouted Mr Hornbrook. 'Scat 'em, Jimmy.'

'What do you mean?' Pauline looked horrified, 'They are baby mice and there's a nest of them. You will leave them alone!'

'Perhaps their mother will come back if we don't interfere,' I suggested. 'We can miss that row of potatoes.' I didn't share Pauline's description of them being sweet and quickly refused her offer to hold them, but I would help in the rescue.

'Leave 'em be. I'll drive over 'em,' Jimmy Coombes ordered.

'You heathen! You beast! You won't!' Pauline fumed, picking up two more, and gently transferring them to her pocket. At that moment Mr Knowles arrived on the scene and stood by Cecil. 'What's the trouble now?' he asked, puzzled.

'Vermut boss. That maid's got 'em in 'er pocket.' Mr Hornbook swung round and glared at Pauline, 'You don't dare carry 'em 'ome, Reg won't like it.' His voice was trembling.

'You! You're scared of mice, mate, aren't you?' Nell faced the old man, 'Don't ever take the Mickey out of us again.'

'Best leave 'em, Pauline,' Cecil said with a smile. 'They baint no good to teddies.'

'I'll not let that heathen kill them.' Pauline was adamant and defiantly walked the length of the field and laid the little pink bodies carefully on the hedge. Coming back to the tractor she looked directly at Mr Knowles: 'In future I shall put every baby mouse I see in a safe place whether you like it or not!' Evidently Mr Knowles was a man of few words. His lips moved slightly and he shook his head twice, then he went back across the field with stick and dog while Cecil gazed at Pauline strangely!

The mist closed in and slowly dampened our macs but we continued to pick up potatoes. The wet earth stuck to them, filling the sacks faster – but what did we care?

'Finish this row and away to the lewth,' Cecil called. 'I'm afeard it won't stop enting down now.'

We walked drearily to the hedge and crouched low.

The wind drove the rain into our faces; in no time we were bedraggled and thoroughly fed up waiting for the lorry to return. This kind of rest wasn't welcomed, it was too wet to smoke!

Eventually the lorry came into sight and Roy was still singing the praises of Old Mother Slipper Slopper! Our angry words halted his merry song.

'Where the bloody 'ell 'ave you been?' Nell dragged her feet in the mud trying to reach the lorry, and as she shouted she slipped. When she got up, one of her wellington boots stayed firmly gripped in the mud. Out of the boot came her stockinged foot and she fell again hitting her face on her tin box. Bunny, close behind, took one look at the muddy heap then carefully skirted the prostrate Nell who was too dumbfounded to swear!

Roy, looking harassed, went to her aid. 'If you'll let me put my arms round you, I'll get you up. Don't look so ugly, maid.'

'It's your fault that she's in the mud,' Jackie scowled. 'If you weren't driving around the countryside singing your bloody head off we would have been home by now. Yes, it's your fault.' Roy opened his mouth to speak but Bunny cut in irritably: 'Roy, for heaven's sake get us home as quick as possible. I am wet and dirty and want a bath. Oh, how filthy wet mud is!'

Nell was hauled into the lorry, her boot and box thrown in after her. I looked at Mr Hornbrook, who once again sat gripping his knees with a grin on his face.

'Oh no, not a live mouse!' I shouted, pointing to his feet. He jumped up and swiftly moved to the other side of the lorry. Yes, Nell was right, this man was afraid of mice!

Reaching Wadebridge an hour earlier than the previous day we decided to meet at the local pub later in the evening. Walking into the bar of the Cornish Arms three hours later we were met by the inquisitive eyes of the few local men already seated there. Nell, having recovered from her muddy ordeal, had regained her spirit and marched straight to the bar ahead.

'A pint please,' she ordered without hesitation.

'A pint of what, miss?' the barman smiled.

'Beer, of course.'

'And your friends?'

'They'll sort themselves out.'

From across the room words reached us. 'My ivers! Invasion, lads.' As we ordered drinks one by one, the men listened to our complaints about the two days we had spent at Tintagel.

'They take 'ee far 'nough away. 'Tis no-man's-land up there,' said a man wearing a cap pushed to the back of his head.

'You're so right, there isn't a man anywhere in sight!' Bunny answered, 'Are there any dances held here in Wadebridge?'

'No, miss, not less any troops come. We got a picture 'ouse tho'.'

'Can any of you sing?' asked a young man dressed in brown corduroy trousers and tweed jacket, 'Bill over there plays piano.'

'Yes, let's sing,' chorused one and all in green jumpers.

Bill took hold of his glass of beer and made for the piano. 'Well, what shall I play?'

We named a number of modern tunes but got the same response each time: 'Don't know it.'

'Then for God's sake play something you do know,' said Jackie.

Bill played a few notes and the locals started harmonizing, 'There is a green hill far away . . .'

'Stop! Stop! We ain't in church.' Nell tried to drown the voices but couldn't. The tune was unfamiliar so we sat and listened. Their voices and tune were well worth listening to. After they sang a second time we were able to join in.

'Now how about Old Mother Slipper Slopper?' asked Bunny.

'That's one of Roy Davey's specials,' Bill grinned. 'He'll teach you if you ask him.'

While we were singing, Nell had ordered and drunk another pint. It seemed as though she could hold her own in any mess tent!

The barman's voice rang out: 'Time please. Ladies, please leave and the gentlemen will follow.'

We said goodnight and went our separate ways,

thinking that maybe Wadebridge wasn't such a bad place after all. And what did Bill mean as he winked to the young man and muttered, 'Sure 'nough, you'll find a shiner 'mongst them lot of maids, me lad. That's if you can compete with the Yanks that they say are coming here soon.'

They? Who were 'they?' Was it true that the Yanks were coming?

Chapter 5

King Arthur's Castle

A MONTH of working in the area of Tintagel, faced with constant mists and rain falling on row upon row of potatoes was enough to dishearten even the robust, so perhaps it was surprising that only two of the gang packed their kitbags and returned to London.

Soon after these girls left, the weather at last turned. The sun shone for days and we were shifted from Tintagel to work in fields just above Polzeath, a long sandy bay of Atlantic surf. At last we could work without macs on, we could take off our heavy green jumpers and even our shirts. Wellingtons were discarded for old shoes, enabling us to roll the legs of our dungarees up above the knees. At long last our skins began to turn a lovely tan, making us feel that at least we had achieved some reward for enduring the long, horrible spell of dampness.

The day came when we were to start a different job. As we sat in the lorry waiting for Roy to make his usual quick get-away, Cecil poked his head round the side.

With a broad grin he said, 'It be something new today, girls – thistle-dodging.' He jumped in the cab leaving us to conjure some weird and wonderful scenarios in which we might be involved with these prickly weeds!

Leaving the lorry, we were faced with a large harvest field in which here and there great patches of corn yet to be harvested because of the wet autumn lay almost flat on the ground.

'Tis sad you, sad.' Cecil turned to Roy: 'Barley gone to lie, 'ealthy field of barley too. You maids will now go through the field and pull up all the thistles you see.'

'What?' Jackie looked appalled, 'I've never pulled a weed up in my life. Why don't you just mow the bloody lot down?'

'You've been a damn good lot for dodging work, now you'll find what the word really means.'

With this remark Roy returned to the lorry, rendering another bout of 'Old Mother Slipper Slopper'. After several orders from Cecil to 'Spread out', girls were scattered among the barley, pulling, bending and popping up above the corn that was still standing. Cries of 'Oh!' constantly rang through the air as the sharp prickles entered our skin and the heads of barley whipped across our faces.

After about an hour's toil, Jackie straightened up with a groan and, with gimlet eye, surveyed the rest of us. Looking at her blistered hands, she wailed, 'To think I only joined the Land Army to get a bleedin' tan! Has anyone got a fag?'

She glanced to and fro at those who happened to be upright and received the same reply, a sad 'No.' Producing a somewhat bent dog-end from an otherwise empty cigarette packet, she lit up and inhaled deeply with satisfaction.

The next moment she let out a piercing scream and leapt into the arms of an unsuspecting Nell who was close by. Nell fell sideways catching her face on a thistle and continued to the ground. Swearing, she tried to get to her feet again, 'What the hell . . .'

'Bloody snakes now!' Jackie's scream had reached full pitch. Snakes? A chill ran down my spine and goose pimples appeared on my arms. I was petrified of snakes – but where were they?

'There it is, you fools!' shrieked Jackie, pointing.

Alarmed, we followed the direction of her trembling finger and perceived a cat picking its way cautiously, tail erect and completely oblivious to us and Jackie's cries of terror. This was too much, we fell to the ground laughing, ignoring Jackie who had turned pale. She was, of course, extremely hurt by our unfeeling reaction and so turned towards Cecil for comfort.

He too had straightened his back quickly and rushed through the barley quite prepared to deal with any number of reptiles. His smile expressed both amusement and exasperation as he shook his head. 'I've 'eard tell of squeamish townies, seems tis true. 'Ow the 'ell you'd make out on a farm I'm damned if I do know. Never seen such a shine in my life.'

While Cecil stood pondering over the confusion Mr Knowles came into the field. It was uncanny that he always showed himself within seconds of a crisis. I began to suspect that he often lurked out of sight waiting for the worst to happen and if it did, deliberately hid until he saw that Cecil had dealt with the disorder. He never showed a glimmer of interest in the commotion that was raised, never asked why we were not working at that particular time, though his blank look would inevitably be cast upon Nell or Jackie. Rubbing her cheek, Nell returned the silent look, waiting for an opening to attack, but she was disappointed. Mr Knowles took a sweeping glance over the field, said his few words to Cecil then vanished out of sight whistling to his little dog.

There was no order in the direction we took as we searched for thistles so it wasn't surprising that we found ourselves going around in circles! Moving to my right I was about to grip a thick green stem when I heard a rustle and saw several stalks move. The tabby cat? Yes, he must be hunting for mice.

'Don't be afraid, Pat, it's only me,' the voice whispered. 'If you sit down low enough you can't be seen. Nice way to rest.' I crawled through the barley on hands and knees towards the whisper. There sat Bunny, her legs crossed. She had renewed her make-up and was now engrossed in plucking her eyebrows!

'Other girls are also hiding,' she smiled. 'As long as we stand up now and then in a different place Cecil won't catch on.' Until lunch time we crawled, we sat, we stood, we moved a few paces and then went into hiding again. It was fun and when the field was finished I would tell Roy that it was 'Cecil-dodging'.

During this warm period we sat on the cliffs and ate our food. In spite of the glorious weather and the sun tans we were acquiring, moans were abundant when our tin boxes were opened. Seagulls hovered then swooped, picking up fish-paste sandwiches, lumps of cheese and the thick pastry ends of pasties. Jackie overcame her fear of them, in fact she was often the first to open her tin, break a sandwich in two and toss it into the air.

It was also the time we got to know each other better through talking about our pre-WLA days. Bunny, our glamour girl, surprised us with her amusing account.

'The reason I was christened Violet could only have been revenge, revenge on the part of my parents because I wasn't born a boy.' Her home was one of the many terraced houses in Peckham Rye. 'My father is a rag-and-bone man with a horse and cart, and every evening the poor animal has to be squeezed through the front door, along the passage and out into the back yard where it's bedded down for the night. There's no other access so there I sit, humiliated to say the least, especially when I'm just getting comfortable on the couch in the front parlour with a boyfriend!'

Pauline came from Woolwich and had worked in an office. She loved animals and had joined the WLA because of this love. Yet here she was, on a cliff top two months later having come into contact with some unfortunate baby mice, Mr Knowles's dog, a fleeting glance of a stray cat and an earlier brief encounter with a few cows being taken from Penzance market!

What seemed to matter most was what part of the capital we had lived in. The majority of the gang hailed from the north of London. Nell was brought up in Paddington; Jackie in Hackney Wick. Kay's home was Finsbury Park while Phyllis's was Holloway. Jimmy came from Acton. My home lay in Dulwich. Each of us was justifiably proud of our 'home town'. The one thing we had in common was a sense of humour, which we badly needed to carry us through the ordeal of yet more continuous potato picking in the days to follow.

Back we went to Tintagel and the rain and mists were with us again. Now it was 'second picking'. Instead of working in rows, we worked across the field in lines. This became even more tedious than picking up freshly dug potatoes for we had to scan the ground looking for small potatoes left behind – also the potatoes that had been stamped into the ground!

One day the sun began to peep from the clouds, so I

suggested we take our food boxes to nearby King Arthur's Castle and explore.

'Yes, let's do that,' agreed Pauline, 'and we might find somewhere to light a fire and cook some potatoes.'

Putting the largest potatoes down the legs of our wellingtons, we left Cecil and Jimmy Coombes and hobbled over to the ruins of the castle. Rambling through the large boulders Peggy spotted a square hole. 'This could have been the oven,' she said. 'Whatever it was it will do for cooking.'

'Okay girls, get cracking and find some wood,' ordered Nell. She was coming into her own again by organizing us.

'I'm too soddin' tired,' grumbled Jackie who promptly sat down, taking a cigarette from her pocket.

In no time we gathered armfuls of bracken and twigs and a fire blazed. A piece of old iron was fixed over the flames and held in position with big stones.

'How do we peel the potatoes?' asked Bunny, ever on the look-out for hygiene and unsure that she wanted to eat in such a primitive fashion.

'Madam, we don't,' Pauline told her. 'Just scrape off the mud.'

Smoke drifted into the air as the potatoes were thrown on the iron. Nell was quite unaware that her face had turned black and her hair was full of grey smuts from the fire.

With a sandwich in one hand and a half-smoked

cigarette in the other, Jackie continued to grumble: 'Bleedin' fish paste again, I'm starving. Wish I was in London having fish and chips.'

Ignoring her, we explored the skeleton of the castle. No one could tell us whether any evidence had been found relating King Arthur to it. Cecil had said the castle belonged to the Dark Ages whereas Roy argued that it was built in the 12th century. Both men agreed that no matter what the era, Tintagel and the surrounding villages and towns were definitely Arthurian country: 'To 'ell with any reasoning, it's there to see.' Arthur – or his myth – fired our imaginations as we pulled rather black potatoes from the fire.

'Someone pass me one,' Jackie asked, but again we ignored her.

'We're all in this together, so get your own,' Nell reminded her.

She walked to the fire and seconds later another scream of terror rang through the ruins and echoed along the cliffs: 'Christ! I've burnt me bleedin' 'and.'

Poor Jackie, no sooner had the blisters healed from thistle-dodging than another lot began to form on her fingers!

'Anyone got a fag?' our patient implored.

She was lucky this time. All who smoked took packets from their pockets, so she had several cigarettes given her with much sympathy! To cheer her we reminded her of all the activity that we had seen going on in Wadebridge. We had even seen the occasional American Jeep pass through the town – surely something was going to happen soon?

Unfortunately, while eating and talking, we hadn't been at all concerned about the weather. It was only when the fire died down and Phyllis mentioned that she felt cold that we cast an eye to the atmospheric change. Tucked down amongst the ruins we hadn't noticed the mist that had rolled in from the sea. Clambering to our feet, we were filled with dismay. The field we had wandered from couldn't be seen either! Making our way in the direction we thought we had come from, we were faced with a hedge that none could climb.

'Cecil! Cecil! Cecil!' shouted eighteen voices in panic.

'Let out one of your screams, Jackie, it's sure to penetrate this bloody fog,' suggested Nell in a shaky voice. The idea went unheeded, Jackie leaned against the hedge holding her hand, not a trace of humour in her expression.

Three more shouts for 'Cecil' rang out but seemed to be caught in the thick Cornish mist and die.

Jackie scowled at me: 'It's all your bleedin' fault, fancy wanting to crawl around old ruins. You're mad, you're a lunatic.' Pauline cupped her hands over her mouth: 'Heathcliff,' she called trying to make light of the situation, 'We are here, Heathcliff!'

A faint whistle permeated the white haze then a

man's voice reached us. Huddled against the hedge we saw the outline of Cecil and his mackintosh; never were we to see him so angry.

'Dammit all, maids, what have 'ee been doing? I called to 'ee 'bout the mist creeping in. Couldn't see sight nor sign of 'ee anywhere. Just 'oped you 'ad some sense, but no, you're plum soft.'

'We've only been examining a part of your lovely Cornish history,' I said. 'King Arthur picked a stupid spot for himself and his knights, didn't he?'

'Bugger the knights and bugger the days, who cares about history anyway? I'm fed up with spuds and fish paste and I've had enough of being cold and wet. All I've got to show for hard work are blisters and baggy trousers cos I've lost weight,' Jackie complained. 'This is the end, I'm leaving the Land Army.'

'Hard work?' Cecil queried from the other side of the hedge. 'Betterfit you 'eld your tongue and stopped straking. Now come along, there be a gateway upalong. If Roy is back 'e'll be in a pretty shape . . . that's if 'ee baint got lost too!'

Groping our way back we were relieved to see that Roy had returned. He was pacing up and down in agitation, his face marked with anxiety. 'I came back early for you and what do I find? Nothing. That's gratitude for you. As for you, Cecil,' he yelled, 'if you want to go hobbling round the fields with them then leave me know afore 'and I'll not 'urry back.'

'Now look here, mate, Cecil found us and . . .'

'Found you? Then I wish to 'ell 'ee would lose you. If you must go on the ran-dan then I'll get you back to Wadebridge in plenty of time to see the bloody Yanks that 'ave arrived!' The wave of temper left Roy as he mentioned the news about Americans, He got into the lorry and Cecil took a few steps away from us and glanced at the left side of the truck. Hearing his sharp intake of breath, Pauline and I followed his gaze, from the cab door to the rear wheel where a long, deep dent explained the real cause of Roy's ill humour: he had been in an accident along the way!

Long before the lorry had reached Wadebridge Jackie's gloom disappeared, she had forgotten her resolve to resign and leave us. On the contrary, she sat making plans with Nell for the evening. When Jackie got down from the lorry when we stopped at the church, her voice exuded happiness and her face expressed anticipated pleasure. 'See you all tonight, girls. The Cornish Arms or even the Molesworth Hotel.' Grabbing her tin box she ran into her billet.

Later that evening Kay and I sauntered down to the bridge to meet the other girls waiting near the level-crossing. Should we go into the Cornish Arms or pay one of our infrequent visits to the Molesworth Hotel? Nell quickly made her decision.

'I'm not going in the Molesworth. I don't like the look of Mrs Crow and I know she doesn't like the look of me, so I'm off to the Cornish Arms, more fun in there. I bet you'll follow me later.'

A dozen of us entered the Molesworth and were greeted with a stony look from Mrs Crow, the proprietress who never seemed to have a cordial welcome for land girls. Apart from half a dozen Americans, the bar was empty; thus we were conspicuous when we entered. Feeling embarrassed by the stares from these Americans, we hesitated by the door.

It was a mistake to dither by this entrance for the door suddenly opened into my back. Stepping to one side, I accepted the apology of one soldier and then another and watched as about thirty Americans filled the room. With curiosity they in turn stood in groups looking at us. It was clear they had never heard of WLA girls let alone seen any dressed in such a uniform. Edging his way nearer to us a young friendly American asked, 'What are you, girls?'

'Land girls,' volunteered Pauline. 'We're from London but are based here to work in the fields while our men are away fighting.' They listened with interest and were amazed that English girls worked on the land. They were even more astonished to learn that we had actually volunteered to do the work. Under the eagle eye of Mrs Crow we carried on talking and learned that these 503rd Engineers had arrived in England from the USA only a few days earlier.

Jackie sat nursing her blistered fingers. Gone were

thoughts of leaving the Land Army, instead she be-moaned the shortage of cigarettes. 'Yeah! We had to queue for fags in London and it ain't much better down here. This is my last one.'

Looking aghast and full of sympathy, the fair-haired Archie slipped his hand to the breast pocket of his tunic, pulled out a pack of Lucky Strike and laid it in front of Jackie. 'Help yourself,' he said.

Still aware of Mrs Crow's eyes fixed on us, Jackie picked up the cigarettes and announced in a loud voice, 'Let's get out of here, there's a better pub across the road.' We filed from the room in twos: Jackie was with her Archie, Kay with Stoney, Pauline with Lee and I was accompanied by Chuck.

We squashed into the Cornish Arms and saw Nell surrounded by soldiers. As the time came to leave, Nell stood up, went to the door and swung around. Letting her eyes sweep over all the Yanks she declared, 'These girls are good girls – so watch it, Yanks!'

Chapter 6

The Christmas Chicken

As the weeks passed so did the potato picking and we found ourselves mending sacks ready for the next potato crop. This job was done in a large building on the quay in Wadebridge. We no longer spent time riding in the lorry, for the quay was only fifteen minutes walk away. However, we refused to continue along Egloshayle road until we had met the post lady and retrieved any letters that were for us. This kind and tolerant woman would lean her bicycle on the curb when she saw any land girls nearing, undo the string from a bundle of mail and wait for us to rush to her. This she did every morning we worked in Wadebridge, then continued on her way ignoring the chagrin and mortified looks that came her way from the inhabitants.

To waste time and evade work wasn't easy; and how to get out of the building on any pretext wasn't easy – unless one 'went sick'. Cecil seemed quite prepared to overlook the late morning arrivals; it was nearly the end of November and the mornings were cold and dark anyway.

We saw Mr Knowles more often. He lived in a large house high on a bank only five minutes from the quay, so he trotted to and fro twice a day with his dog. Conversation from him was, as usual, almost nil. He would take a sweeping look over the girls who sat huddled on bundles of sacks slowly working with large steel needles and string, turn his back and proceed to write something in a little book. After he left us we would watch him walk over the bridge, hesitate for a few moments as if contemplating which direction to take next, then carry on over the level-crossing and up the main street.

'Where the 'ell does that man go, Cecil? For a pint?' Nell asked one morning.

'No, maid, now that 'ee want to know I'll tell 'ee. He comes by and notes how many maids go missing of a sudden.' Cecil held a steel needle in mid-air for a second and then pushed it into the gathered sacking. 'There baint a day passes without one of you skiving and saying they be ill or summat, twadden as if you be out in the wind and rain now. 'E'll be mazed if it carries on.'

Jackie had unconsciously started our routine visits to the local doctor. With blistered fingers she had reported to him and then related her story to us one evening.

'It's easy, girls, dead easy, if you want time off. When he asked how I'd burnt my fingers I told 'im straight that we were starving and tried to cook some potatoes at Tintagel cos the bloody seagulls ate our food. He was shocked, mates, and asked me if I wanted to get out of

76

the WLA. He don't believe in girls working on the land and I've got a certificate to 'ave a week off.'

From then on the doctor had frequent visits from all of us! In turn he dealt with backaches, earaches, an epidemic of colds induced by pepper-filled handkerchiefs and one honest case of continual nose-bleeds!

'So if you don't want to get caught out, you best stay away from this end of town,' Cecil warned what remaining fit girls there were listening. ''E's out tracking maids roaming around.'

Whether we roamed or went to work, none were too tired to go to the regular dances that were now being held in Wadebridge. Our concern had switched to the problem of what to wear with our breeches. When money and clothing coupons allowed, we spent an occasional Saturday afternoon in Bodmin buying cheap blouses. As Christmas leave wasn't so very far away it wouldn't be long before we had our 'civvies' with us. Until then, a great deal of swapping took place, and to make our wardrobes look more extensive, pyjama tops were improvised as extra blouses!

With only a week to go before our first leave we thanked the post lady for our letters and carried on towards the quay. Coming up fast behind us was Roy and his lorry. Skidding to a halt, he yelled from the cab window, 'Get in girls, 'nother new job today. You're off to St Breward to pull up carrots, so make it sharp.'

Not daring to agitate Roy when he had our life in his hands, I pushed the letter I had received from my brother into my pocket, crossed the road and jumped up with the 'Egloshayle girls'. Cecil had already been informed about the work to be done and was waiting with the rest of the gang. Counting, and finding a full attendance, his smile beamed into the lorry, 'Good, good, proper job. Tis cold but sun should break through later.'

As on the previous journeys towards 'The Blessed Country', the name we had given to this northern part of Cornwall that had so many Saint prefixes, we passed small, familiar villages before veering to the right. The lorry jerked down a long and bumpy lane where it was impossible to light a cigarette and nearly hopeless to talk.

I remembered my letter and took it from my pocket. My brother, who was training to be a pilot, had returned the empty work time-sheet that I had sent him but now it was filled with his own humorous ideas on how we spent our working hours. Kay read it with me and then it was passed to Pauline. No sooner had she glanced at the heading than the lorry bumped to a halt. Shivering, we jumped from the lorry onto hard-frozen earth. Instantly the coldness penetrated the soles of our wellington boots and passed up our legs.

'Oh my God, it's like Siberia,' Jackie trembled. 'You sure you ain't lost us, Roy? And look! There's that bloody Brown Willy again.'

We looked. This was a different view of the famous and ominous range of hills, we were now on the western edge of Bodmin Moor.

'What fool planted carrots out here?' Nell asked, bewildered.

'And what fool thinks we're going to pull them up?' Kay added. Both Cecil and Roy were stamping up and down the rows trying to kick up the earth. It wouldn't budge, so what were we to do?

'Baint no good till the ground eaves, Roy. Tis too cold for you to sit in the lorry, maids,' Cecil turned to face eighteen miserable girls. 'Tell 'ee what, go for a walk over to St Breward church on the 'illtop there.'

There was no choice! With faces buried into chests to ward off the icy wind we made our way over the rock-strewn moor and along a pathway that led to the church that was only partly screened by trees. A small village lay on the level below the church. Not a movement could be seen.

Pauline opened the door of the church and we filed in quietly. 'Keep your voices down and no swearing.' she warned softly.

'But it's bl—, it's freezing in here too!' whispered Nell.

'Let's keep moving and look around. It's more interesting than Brown Willy and carrots,' I said with enthusiasm.

'You lot! First castles and now bl—, and now

churches.' Jackie pulled a packet of Lucky Strike from her pocket as she moaned. While she sat turning the packet over and over in her hand Kay went up the aisle, sat down at the organ and began to play a Christmas carol. Bunny and Grace had disappeared into the vestry but as Kay continued to play on the organ they appeared looking very solemn wearing the choir boys' cassocks!

'Sing, Jackie, sing,' Nell ordered. 'You'll forget you're cold.'

Doris had climbed into the pulpit and was blathering something about the art of picking up potatoes and the skill in avoiding doing so!

'Hey, Pat, give Doris your time sheet, let her read it from the pulpit for a laugh,' Kay called to me. I took the sheet and handed it to Doris then sat back in the pew beside Jackie.

'If you want to go outside and smoke,' I told her, laughing, 'now is the time. If you want a giggle, stay.'

Doris raised the sheet of white paper, cleared her throat and her first loud words echoed in the church: 'Opinion Censored.'

As Doris neared the end of the time sheet the church door opened and there stood the local vicar. He seemed pleased to see quite a congregation and walked up to the pulpit and Doris.

'Tell me what you are reading, please?' he smiled.

'I daren't!'

'Why?'

Cornwall War Agricultural Executive Committee

Opinion Censored,

Enjoyment ~~TIME~~ SHEET

Name _Davis May (Pat)_ Week ending ~~Never~~ begins 19 43

Date ~~Last Calendar~~	Hours	Name and ~~Address~~ Homeless of Farmer	Full Details of work ~~whats this~~	Hours ~~worked~~ to be entered in in figures and certified by farmer
Monday	8	I.M.A. Pig	Laying on the Haystack	8 hours, Cows ate hay causing no overtime and Rig
Tuesday	8	A. Turnip top	buddling the Cows.	8 hours. Cows got fed up so no overtime a Turnip top
Wednesday	0	Teddy B. gexes	Picking up Spuds.	0 hours never saw w.L.A. Today Teddy Big eyes.
Thursday	12	Max Factor	Making up face.	12 hours plus 4 hours overtime. Max Factor
Friday	24	L.O.T.S Long-Snores	Sleeping	24 hours guaranteed. L.O.T.S Long-Snores
Saturday	24	Big Ben	On Strike	24 hours - never heard the chimes Big Ben.
Sunday	12	A. Yankee Doodle	O.T with Yanks	12 hours. this is questionable. A Yankee Doodle.

Signed ~~the Elzsabeth~~. Certified Correct I darent

Date God knows. 19 43.

havent found calendar

'God knows!'

'Do you know what day it is?'

'Haven't found the calendar yet!'

Hearing this last remark the perplexed vicar glanced at us as we sat silent in the pews. His eyes strayed to our wellington boots and recognition spread across his face.

'Ah, land girls. What work brings you to St Breward, then?'

'Carrots. The bl—, the things are frozen in the ground,' said Nell.

'Have you been here before?'

'No,' we replied in unison.

'Then if you do visit us again may I suggest something? May I propose that you bring your time-table of recreation with you. I will pray that one of you will have the courage to recite the contents. As only the Lord and yourselves know who composed the document and caused such laughter, I will also pray to be enlightened.' The vicar's blue eyes smiled as he went on, 'As the year is almost over it is hardly worth the effort of searching for a calendar is it? I wish you all a peaceful Christmas, girls.'

As we left the church Doris handed me back the sheet. I knew the vicar had seen the transaction so I handed it to him to read. 'Thank you, my dear. I heard the beginning, now I've seen the end!'

★   ★   ★

At last! Nearly four months after joining the WLA we stood waiting for the train at Wadebridge station, going home for our first leave. With only five minutes to go a commotion reached our ears and Nell's voice rose above the din. As she approached the train we could see she had a sack slung over her shoulder and whatever was in the sack was putting up a struggle. While she bowled along, a picture of happiness, oblivious to the fact that she was now the centre of everyone's attention, we could only stand and wait, open mouthed!

'I've got me Christmas dinner wiv me. Fancy! A bleedin' live chicken, mates.' Nell spoke as if the heavens had fallen in her lap. 'Me old man will be pleased.'

'He might be but we ain't. Don't sit near me with the bloody thing,' Jackie told her scornfully.

Nell looked at us. 'Who will sit with me, then?'

'Nobody but Pauline,' I told her, 'She loves animals, as you know.'

'Right then, Pauline, follow me.' Nell hopped onto the train, swung the sack up on the luggage rack with no difficulty then turned and pulled Pauline in beside her. The chicken made a violent effort to get free, emitting even louder clucks and squawks!

Succumbing to Nell's request for company, Pauline sat on the edge of her seat unhappily watching the wriggling bird while Nell, quite unperturbed, sat back, lit a cigarette and confided, 'Got it from this old farmer, a real live chicken for only five bob!' Scrambling into another nearby compartment I caught sight of Mr Knowles, his stick raised in farewell. Yet again he had witnessed a mêlée and stayed in hiding until it had passed!

Plymouth. As with the journey down it meant refreshments, and when the train pulled in Nell was quick to be the first on the platform. 'You stay where you are,' she called back to Pauline. Guard the chicken in case it gets nicked. I'm off to find a couple of Yanks to buy us some food. Don't look so shocked!' Pauline, full of doubt about sitting underneath a squawking chicken all the way to London, became even more dubious about the finding of Yanks but was afraid to say No.

Within ten minutes Nell's mission had been accomplished. She boarded the train with two pugnacious looking Americans, picked the most presentable one for herself and then steered the way to the buffet car. Kay and I watched the manoeuvre from the corridor. We heard Pauline accept the hospitality with thanks and embarrassment while Nell, as always completely unselfconscious, deemed it her divine right!

The two Americans got off at Reading and Nell was all for finding replacements to provide her with tea. This was too much for Pauline and her angry words carried to where we sat. 'Take your choice, either you let me buy tea or bloody well sit there by yourself with your damned chicken, I've had enough!' Silence! Nell had at last given in to Pauline's objections!

At Paddington, Nell came into her own again. With the sack slung over her shoulder she followed Pauline to the barrier where Pauline's sister, Lorna, was waiting for her. Having heard about Lorna and the shock she got when she heard Pauline had joined the WLA, we stood back to watch the encounter. Pauline introduced the two girls, then stepped aside apprehensively.

'Wotcha cock!' Nell thumped Lorna on the back. 'Come and have a pint, I'll treat yer for Christmas.'

Lorna straightened her coat and put on a brave smile. The three girls disappeared out of Paddington station with the 'bleedin' chicken' still squawking while the rest of us went our separate ways.

Chapter 7

A Prayer of Despair

MID January. The weather determined whether we continued to repair potato sacks in Wadebridge or carried out the only alternative task, carrot pulling. Harsh winds added to incessant rain and we were grateful for shelter though this was not enough to stem the moans of 'Just like bloody Dartmoor.'

Cecil had become resigned to hearing constant grumbles and did his best to combat the boredom by telling us some of the history of Wadebridge. 'The bridge be one of the best in Cornwall. There was this 'ere Lovebone, the vicar of Wadebridge who put it in fair shape with some good people 'elping 'im. I hear tell Lovebone almost despaired when the arches was first set on the quick-sandy ground, then 'e took 'eart when he laid packs of wool for foundation.

'Used to be a little chapel at each end. Then along comes Cuthbert Mayne who was a priest and acted as chaplain to someone of the old faith. 'E was dragged to prison and 'is body was torn in pieces while 'e still lived.

Poor beggar. Part of 'is body was fixed on Wadebridge. Cromwell 'as also been 'ere and you tell me you've never 'eard tell of it before?'

'Give over, Cecil,' Jackie would say as he was about to carry on imparting more general information. 'We want to talk about Yanks!'

'You be seeing others different to Yanks today,' Cecil told us one sunny morning. 'Roy will be 'ere in a minute and you be all going to St Merryn, the Fleet Air Arm is over there.'

'Sailors? So what?' shrugged Nell to indicate her lack of interest.

The journey wasn't too far and as we neared St Merryn green fields could be seen stretching to the sand dunes and the sea. At least for this day we would not be exposed to bleak moors. Leaving Bunny in the lorry to finish making up her face we got out and looked around, amazed to see we were in the middle of an airfield!

'My God, what have we come here for?' asked Pauline aghast.

'Don't panic, just follow me,' Cecil smiled. 'Remember that you are here to work. If you bear that in mind there won't be any trouble.'

As we walked across a large stretch of grass, we could see aeroplanes taking off and coming in to land from different directions.

Up and over a small bank and there were the carrots.

There was also a wide path of tarmac – we were at the side of a runway!

'Don't be 'urried girls, the planes won't be flying this way,' Cecil said confidently. 'Though I 'spect you wish they were!'

Apart from the occasional glance at flying aircraft we worked steadily feeling pleased that the carrots left the ground without too much tugging. And then it happened! What had been a small black speck in the sky loomed nearer, larger and lower.

'Christ! I swear— DUCK!' Nell didn't finish. We were flat on our stomachs frightened and waiting . . . waiting for what? As the drone of the engine receded, one by one we sat up more than a little dazed, only to see Cecil running for his cap.

'Tis all right, maids, the pilot couldn't 'ave known we were 'ere,' Cecil tried to calm us. Believing him, we picked up the scattered carrots and carried on working. Half an hour later our stomachs hit the ground again!

'It's bloody suicide staying here, so I'm leaving,' Nell raved.

'Did you see the pilot wave?' asked Bunny shakily.

'No, but I'll see the bastard dead,' said Nell walking away. Wanting to back Nell, we picked up our tin boxes and followed. Ignoring Cecil's protests we started to walk across the large area of grass again, wondering where to go for safety.

'We can't leave Cecil on his own,' I said. 'It's not his fault.'

'He's not on his own, he's got the best of the bloody lunatics in the Navy watching over him! Work and there won't be trouble, he says. Well, if dive bombing ain't trouble mates . . .' Nell stopped to catch her breath and while doing so clenched her hand into a fist, 'Just let me get at them. God! Down we go again.' Like a small flock kneeling in reverence we sank to the ground for the third time and waited for the swooping aircraft to pass over. When we rose from the ground Cecil was at our side again.

'Gesson back to where Roy dropped 'ee, I'm off to report they buggers. Can't abide to be taken on the ground hop.' Cecil tightened the string that held his old fawn raincoat together, gave his cap a couple of twists, making sure the peak was well and truly in the correct place, and then made his way towards a grey building in the distance, muttering that the whole morning had been 'a pretty take'.

It was well over an hour before Cecil returned, his face lit with a victorious smile. 'They be having reprimand for this, girls. Sure 'nough they won't come nist us again, that I do know.'

'I don't care what they are having and I don't care where they are going,' said Jackie lighting a cigarette from the butt of another, 'I'm not going back to that runway, none of us are.'

89

'But they carrots are wanted,' Cecil's voice was begging.

'Then get the bleedin' Fleet Air Arm to blow them out.'

'Here comes Freddie Knowles, he'll sort it out,' said Cecil, twisting and lifting his cap.

I watched the little man approach to within a few yards of us. He looked from Cecil to Bunny, who was combing her hair, and then he gazed blankly up to the empty sky. Yes, he had seen the flying performance but had only shown his presence when some semblance of order reigned! He hovered near Cecil, obviously wondering what our next move was going to be. Before he had appeared our minds had been made up – to get off the airfield and wait for Roy. Could he now assert his authority and risk open rebellion?

'These maids are 'urried I can tell 'ee,' Cecil continued to twist and lift his cap around his head. 'When we get a scat of dryth and they work 'ard what happens? They damned sailors fly low down werratting 'em. Some job it be, some job.'

'It's also the sum total of the work we're doing today,' Pauline faced Mr Knowles. 'We've all got stomach aches, haven't we?'

Hearing this remark about the state of our anatomies, Mr Knowles's face flushed pink and he glanced down at his stick.

'As you wish. Tomorrow you'll go to a farm at St

Teath.' The words left his mouth quietly and quickly and in the same manner he turned and strode away from the airfield leaving us to idle the time away until Roy picked us up. We walked down to the sea and dunes with no pains whatsoever in mind or body!

St Teath and our first farm. The lorry swayed down a rough lane and stopped near a long low farmhouse. The walls and roof of the building were of the same substance, grey cement, and had an air of poverty. A large mound of dung lay only a few yards away and a few chickens pecked and scratched at the edge of the mound.

Nell stared with horrified eyes as the chickens sorted through pieces of dirty straw, found nothing so hopped further into the heap of dung, scattering it in all directions. She put her hand to her mouth as if to be sick, clearly remembering her Christmas dinner! With a shudder she turned, 'No wonder me old man said it stank to 'igh 'eaven and chucked the thing in the dustbin. Christ! The poor things are being starved.' Unlatching her tin Nell took out two sandwiches and threw them towards the chickens. Above the squawks and fluttering of wings in pursuit of the bread a gruff voice reached us from over a nearby hedge. It was obviously the farmer.

'Hey, three of you maids, give us an 'and in 'ere.' A stick was being waved in the air to indicate the position of the unseen being. 'Go downalong, the gate's abroad,' the surly voice added.

'What the 'ell is he doing in there? I'm not going anywhere, I can hear noises. There's bleedin' animals over that hedge so I'm off into the lorry.' With this Jackie jumped into the cab. Cecil peered over the hedge and announced, 'Pigs.'

'Lovely,' Pauline's face brightened. 'Pigs won't hurt anyone.' She stepped forward and Jimmy and I followed, picking our way through thick mud and other small piles of dung. Reaching the gateway of the small meadow we were alarmed to see even larger and deeper patches of mud. Seven pigs stood stubbornly watching us from the other side of the horrible, stinking area.

'Get behind the beasts and send 'em out,' ordered the farmer. 'Plough through it, damn 'ee. Stank around and you'll get bedded in it.' He alluded to the mire we found hard to cross.

With just a couple of yards to go to the opening, the large pigs caught sight of some of the gang who had decided to brave the mud and observe this swinish operation. All came to a halt.

'What's on now?' bellowed the farmer who hadn't yet seen the other girls and expected some kind of a reply.

'Everything's all right, some more girls have come to help,' I told him. 'They aren't really afraid.'

'Shut your mouth,' he snapped at me. 'Best if you'd

stayed with they fools.' Taking a deep breath and raising his head high into the air he started to shout to the unseen girls. 'Get the 'ell away, what do 'ee think you're playing at. Bloody land girls.' He looked straight at me: 'Get the 'ell out of 'ere before the sows drop their young uns. You too,' he said swinging round to Jimmy. 'You're nothing but pests, both of 'ee. Pests!'

'Pests?' I queried, freeing my left boot from the mud with a nasty squelch only to find the right one gripped tightly in the muck! It did nothing to ease my temper. Stuck in the deep mud I looked from Pauline to Jimmy. They didn't understand, either!

'If there's a plague around then you've caused it and if you send your pigs and chickens to the shops then you'll be the cause of food poisoning too. You! You're the reason we're here anyway, if you hadn't wanted us to pick up carrots. . . .' I stopped. Carrots? Then why in heaven's name was I stuck here with seven pigs and a dirty, irate farmer? It was Pauline's fault. Yes, her love for animals had got me in this predicament and now her back was turned on me, all her attention riveted on the pigs which refused to move – and without help, neither could I!

'Galvanize! Iss, galvanize will 'elp,' boomed the farmer. 'Cecil, chuck some over the 'edge then come and tend these teasy maids.' The crash of falling metal frightened the pigs, their legs tottered but with lunge they took off at a trot to the other side of the meadow.

'Damn and blast! The War Office at Truro told me I'd be getting some fitty 'elp and what 'ave I got?' the farmer raged as he set off in pursuit. 'I'll tell 'ee what I've got! A bloody army of lubber 'eaded fools who'm no good to man or beast.' While he and Pauline raced after the pigs, Jimmy and Cecil helped me on to the galvanized iron sheeting and through the gateway where we stayed to watch the hot-tempered farmer and our cool, calm land girl. All eyes were on Pauline and we listened as she called to the pigs in a soft, sweet voice, her hand outstretched and beckoning. 'Come on now, do behave yourselves.'

'Listen, maid, you'll get nowhere with your blubbering. Take a stick and belve at 'em,' the farmer snarled.

'No I won't, how can you be so cruel?'

'Cruel, maid? It's you or them – and by God it'll be them! Bring 'em on, I'd lief look at them as you. Women! Bah!'

They came nearer and into the mud again and we backed away but before we were out of sight Pauline bent to touch one of the pigs. It quickly rounded on her and she crashed into the mud.

'Well I never! How infuriating,' she coolly remarked as she rose from the ground, disregarding the filthy state she was in.

'You're not the least bit good, join the rest of 'em screaming paddicks. You're all outlanders. Whoever heard tell of mollycoddlin' pigs? I ask 'ee!' the farmer continued to grumble, 'Cummus on, Cecil, give us 'and. They bloody girls are useless.' Cecil picked up the dirty piece of galvanize lying near the gateway and plodded through the mud, determination on his face.

'Get on, you buggers,' he yelled, pushing the galvanize into the backs of the pigs, 'you'll not floor me.'

The pigs were almost level with the opening when Bunny stepped forward. 'Ah,' she said, 'so you're a bully too, Cecil!' Hearing the voice the animals huddled together and let out a series of grunts then immediately backed into Cecil. He went sprawling into the mud, the galvanize crashing onto his legs.

'You buggers,' he exploded scrambling to his feet, 'you damn buggers. Scat me down in your own muck would 'ee. I'm lagged in mud but you're going through this 'ere gateway. By God you are.'

Once again the farmer ignored another unpleasant encounter with the mud. He rushed through the gateway, grabbed Bunny by the arm and pushed her towards us. His face was scarlet as he spluttered, 'You may be a fitty looking maid but you've not a happard of sense in 'ee. As for the rest of you lot standing around grizzling like badgers, the sooner you're off my land the better.' He joined Cecil, rattled the metal with his stick and let out a throaty shout. The pigs trotted quietly out and into a grey, cemented sty. The two men returned, Cecil limping badly.

'Knew I could do it on my own, don't need no

army.' The farmer's face crumpled to half a smile, 'Now, Cecil, take your whole kit and get they carrots out the ground before the war gets over.'

'Another bleedin' slave driver,' said Jackie from the cab seat of the lorry. She and Roy had sat listening to and watching the dirty proceedings. Deputizing for Mr Knowles, I thought! And why had Nell kept so quiet? The answer lay in her stomach. She was still clutching it, recalling how near she had been to eating a cheap five-bob chicken!

The bellowing voice directed Roy to the carrot field and as the lorry pulled away the farmer hitched up the dirty sacking that was tied around his waist. 'And see,' he yelled after us, 'that you close 'ome the gate after 'ee.'

Roy didn't leave us, instead he gave Pauline a helping hand. Tearing handfuls of grass from the hedgerow he wiped the mud from the back of her clothes then carefully scraped her dungarees with his penknife, smiling as he moved the small blade.

'You're a right 'eller for animals, aren't you?' Roy's smile broadened, 'maybe this will stop you from taffling with pigs. 'Eller for the turf too, on your belly yesterday and on your back today. God, Pauline, you'll never be a saint!' he guffawed. Mustering what dignity she had, Pauline stomped away from him and joined us. Tight-lipped, she pulled at the carrots furiously.

'Only two more rows and then we be off.' Cecil's

Pat's last day at school, August 1939. She was photographed
by her Dad in Crystal Palace Road, south London.

Kay *(on the left of the picture)* and the author in working overalls
at Wadebridge in 1943.

The author *(left)* and Kay in uniform.

Seventeen members
Back row from the left: Doris, Peggy, Jimmy, unknown, unknown.
Front row: Anne, Sue, Jackie,

of the 'gang' in 1944.
Middle row: Gladys, unknown, unknown, Kay, unknown, Peggy.
Bunny, the author, Pauline.

So that's where my hat went!

Our glamour girl, 'Bunny'.

The author *(left)* with Pauline in 1944.

After the war: the author's husband,
Gordon, at Camborne Cattle Show.

The easiest job on the farm
– 'Gurlyn', April 1946.

Feeding baby hedgehogs at Gurlyn farm.

Reunion photographs from 1961 – eighteen years after we first met.
Top photograph, from the left: Jackie, Kay, Joe Pascoe, the author, Mrs Pascoe.
Bottom photo: Kay, Jackie, the author, Pauline.

words were accompanied by the mooing of cows. We looked around uneasily as the sounds came increasingly near. Jackie's piercing cry and swift disappearance behind a sack of carrots alerted us. Half a dozen brown cows slowly entered the field but for us there was no means of escape! They advanced, heedless of panicky screams.

'Don't be 'urried, girls. Me and Roy will see 'em out. Be still.'

'Blundering army! You left the gate abroad on purpose. Watch the cows stank all over me carrots would 'ee?' The farmer's spate of anger halted the cows, allowing Roy and Cecil to dash forward with arms raised forcing the animals to do an about-turn and make a lively exit. As the last cow passed out of sight the farmer brought a heavy stick down against his boot with temper.

'Now you lot, make 'aste and bugger off my land,' he raged.

'Cummus on, girls, this is the out of it.' Cecil looked at his watch, then faced the farmer, 'You be paying for full time, that will make you uglier still. Missed your 'and there!'

The farmer raised his eyes to the sky. 'Dear God,' he prayed, 'I'm in agony. Why did you send this lot to me? Must be something better at the War Office. Lord, these are nort but poor trade.' Seeing our smiles he vented the last of his fury: 'God damn 'ee, get the 'ell into that bloody lorry and be off!'

Chapter 8

Nell's Birthday

WE were sent back to the Blessed Country and odd remote fields. Not a word, no sign at all from either Cecil or Mr Knowles had been given that several more acres of potatoes had been lying dormant throughout the winter waiting for the frosts to clear before they could be lifted from the ground. Totally ignorant about the way the elements could affect farming and crops, we were lulled into a false sense of security that the potato crop was to be forgotten, at least until months ahead. Cecil's summing up of the time scale also proved to be incorrect and deflated our morale even further.

'The teddies will only take a day or two,' he had informed us optimistically, yet here we were, into a third week and still spud bashing. Patriotism wasn't riding very high amongst us, in fact we had learnt 'The Star Spangled Banner' weeks ago and often, as we passed the American camp on our way home from work, our voices would loudly sing the US anthem. Only when the days were dry and sunny did we salute our own absent men in song.

On such days Roy would sense our mood and as the lorry neared the camp he would keep his hand on the horn signalling our approach until we burst into song, singing loud and clear that 'There'll Always Be an England'. This always brought smiles and waves from the people of Wadebridge whereas the melodious praises of America caused a turning of backs, both lorry and land girls being ignored!

When we arrived home from work one evening Mrs Gill stopped Kay in the hall. 'There be a parcel for you,' she said, 'from America.'

With eyes shining Kay thanked her and ripped off the brown paper revealing a large blue and silver box, emblazoned with the words 'Evening In Paris' across the top. The attached note held belated Christmas greetings to Kay from Stoney's Mom. Such luxury! Not only a large bottle of perfume, but talcum powder and soap, rouge and lipstick lay snuggled on the white satin. Feeling like a filmstar and holding the box in both arms, Kay climbed the stairs to the bedroom and gently laid it on the dressing table. She lifted the lid again and we both sniffed the fragrant aroma, not daring to touch it with our dirty hands.

'Let's have a bath and cover ourselves with the talc,' said Kay. 'You can use the perfume, Pat, only a little, don't forget.' Going downstairs for the evening meal dressed in civvies we felt more like females than we had for months and began to wish there was a dance that evening instead of just a casual stroll around the town or along by the river.

As always, Louis Gill sat alone at his little round table near the bay window with his dog at his feet. As we entered the room he looked up from the scones he was smothering with jam and cream, made his usual cursory inspection of us, emitted a couple of customary 'Mmms', then carried on eating.

Although Mr Gill said little to Kay and me, we were acutely aware that nothing much missed his gaze and he listened silently with great attention to our conversation with Mrs Gill who sat at the larger table with us. She would break the conversation now and then, look over to her husband and ask, 'Did you hear that, Father?' She was rewarded with a nod and a longer 'Mmm' for an answer.

On this particular evening his eyes wandered to the window more than usual, then he craned his neck. Something had evidently caught his attention! Wiping the moustache that completely obliterated his top lip he reached for the binoculars that always lay nearby on a chair. He scanned the far bank of the river that ran the length of Egloshayle road. Letting out a series of 'Mmms', he stood up with agitation.

'What is it, Louis?' asked Mrs Gill anxiously.

'Mmm! It be those damn buggering land girls again, Sarah.'

Kay and I jumped up wondering why our pals were being damned. Following his gaze we saw Sue and Ann picking primroses. Why on earth should this old man be so angry because of this?

'They are only picking flowers for their mothers,' I protested.

'Be the ruination of the countryside,' he scowled at me. ''Tis sad I tell 'ee, Sarah; tis sad the day they came.'

'Hush, Father, do,' replied Mrs Gill, before running from the room. This dear old lady seemed to spend all her time running. If she wasn't running to and from the kitchen, then she ran to the calls of 'Sarah' that all too often came from Mr Gill. She ran down to the shops and ran to the library van that stopped by the post office. Many a time Mrs Gill would cover up for Kay and me when we came in later than the given time. We would creep in the front door as quietly as possible but our footsteps were always heard and brought a shout from the bedroom above.

'Sarah, what time be it?' Mrs Gill would knock half an hour off the clock. 'It's only 11 pm Father, the girls be all right.' We were being confronted by a man who wasn't exactly overjoyed at having two land girls billeted upon him. It was clear from the moment we arrived at Wadebridge that this man, along with other old-timers, had no time for us. We were, in their eyes, 'a band of girls up to no good!' Often after our meals at home Mr Gill would push a cigarette into a holder, balance it between his teeth and sit back with thumbs tucked into his waistcoat, then study us in silence. Intermittent 'Mmms' frequently accompanied a half-smile, which merely amused Kay and me, causing us to ask innocently if he was alright, or 'Did you say something, Father?'

'You girls be going out again tonight, ay?' he asked, though in fact it was a statement. Before we had a chance to answer, an American truck drew up outside the house with a screech of brakes and Meg, clad in breeches and brown stockings, appeared over the tail-end.

'What be on now, Sarah?' Mr Gill rose from his chair quickly and glared out of the window. 'Godammit! Land girls in a lorry again and it be an American lorry, Sarah. What's on?'

Eager to find out just that I rushed from the room and fled down the garden path with Kay close behind, fully aware that Mr Gill watched our every move and was within hearing distance. Nell didn't care who was within hearing distance as she hung from the rear of the truck, shouting her excited orders.

'Come on you two. There's a dance at Bodmin and these Yanks are taking us. Get your bleedin' coats on and hurry.'

Going back indoors we made a rapid dash past the front room, grabbed our coats and whispered to Mrs Gill who was hovering in the passage: 'We shan't be late, you needn't wait up for us.' Safely in the back of the truck, Kay, Nell and I looked at the bay window, smiled at the open-mouthed old man, then waved to him until we were out of his view.

There were already six land girls in the truck. The driver carried on down Egloshayle road and was directed by Nell when to stop next. She thumped on the cab partition and bawled at the top of her voice, 'Two more mates here, cock.' Fourteen of the gang were collected and the truck spun around by the bridge and speeded up towards the church on its way to Bodmin. When we passed our billet we saw Mr Gill standing in his gateway with a cigarette and holder held tightly between his teeth. The driver tooted his horn, which brought a sad shake of Mr Gill's head.

We hadn't gone more than a few miles when there was a nasty hissing sound followed by a rumble coming from underneath the lorry. Within seconds Nell was frantically thumping on the cab.

'Stop the bloody lorry, mate. The wheel's falling off. Stop!'

The lorry stopped and like a flash Nell jumped over the tail-end and began examining the wheels.

'Take it easy, honey,' she was told by one of the Americans. 'It's only a puncture, we'll soon have it fixed. Get back in.'

'Where's the spare wheel, mate?' Nell was fully pre-pared to organize this operation now! Without another word the soldier picked her up and put her back in the truck telling her very firmly to 'Calm down!' She muttered something about going in a bleedin' taxi but she was really more abashed at being unceremoniously placed back in the truck!

On reaching the dance hall Nell couldn't resist giving yet another command. 'We're leaving here at ten-thirty sharp and I don't want any arguments!'

Inside the large hall there were several tables at one end. Arrayed on the tables was an assortment of sandwiches and cakes and bowls of both tinned and fresh fruit. Dotted here and there on the edges of the tables were tumblers full of cigarettes. Not since the war had started had we seen such a display of food. Then we spotted the birthday cake. For whom?

The dance was in full swing and then the band stopped. The GIs started to sing 'Happy Birthday to You.' We looked around then heard, 'Happy birthday dear NE-ELL.' We, her workmates hadn't a clue that it was her birthday but these American soldiers had found out and had done something about it! Tears came to this so-called tough cockney girl.

Although Nell had been temporarily overcome with emotion, she hadn't forgotten to keep her eye on the clock.

'It's time to go, girls,' she shouted round the hall. 'And come on you fellers who are going to Wadebridge, get that lorry rolling. We'll be in trouble after eleven o'clock.'

As we left the dance hall each of us was given a bottle of champagne which we held on to carefully. Arriving back at Wadebridge shortly after our curfew time, Kay and I jumped down from the truck. Crash! My bottle of champagne slipped from my arm and glass shattered over the road. Upstairs windows were thrown open, including Mr Gill's.

'Sarah!' The name rang through the air and brought Mrs Gill rushing to the window, 'It's those damn land girls again I tell 'ee. Dammit, Sarah, they'll have to go.'

'Hush Father, they be up to no harm and they be back early.'

Mrs Gill's voice was meant to soothe but this only incensed Mr Gill more. Holding onto the window ledge with one hand and the other tucked around his nightshirt he bawled, 'They get up late, they come in late, and 'tween times the damn Yanks run amuck besting whether to come or go. I tell 'ee, Sarah, if I could coose them all out of Wadebridge right now I would. War or no, a body needs sleep.'

'But Father, 'tisn't late and they are helping to win the war,' Mrs Gill said, trying to placate her husband.

'Mmm! They couldn't win a toss, leave alone a war. Land girls? Yanks? 'Tis sad, Sarah. Sad!'

While the old man was attacking our feeble war effort Kay and I crept along the path and opened the front door. The truck pulled away and we listened to shouts from the Americans bidding Mr Gill 'Goodnight Sir!' to be immediately followed by the same voices singing, 'For He's A Jolly Good Fellow'. Halfway up the stairs we were confronted with a very angry looking Mr Gill who now stood by his bedroom door bare-footed.

'We really don't want the champagne, do we Kay?' I whispered. She turned to me, quickly grasped my meaning and winked. Stepping forward she swiftly put her bottle into Mr Gill's arms, at the same time wishing him 'Sweet dreams.'

Before he could reply we rushed up to our attic bedroom and closed the door. We sat on the bed and burst out laughing for we were left with the vision of an old man in a striped nightshirt clutching a bottle of champagne with his mouth wide open!

Chapter 9

Baa Baa Black Sheep

IT was a gloriously sunny spring morning and as we sat by the church waiting for the lorry, Mr Knowles drove up and stopped a few yards from us. Leaving his car he crossed the road and stood on the grass verge poking the ground with his stick. As far as we knew it was to be another day at St Issey but now that he had appeared any direction could be expected. Not until Roy drew to a screeching halt alongside the church did the little man cross the road and speak. Tapping Pauline on the shoulder and pointing his stick at me he said, 'I want you two to come with me. You are going to drive some sheep from Camelford to Tintagel. It's only about six miles, let's hope you're capable.'

Pauline and I looked at each other. Capable? Of course we were! As we neared Camelford the silence between us was at last broken.

'I chose you because you seem to have more sense than the rest,' Mr Knowles told Pauline, ignoring my presence in the back of the car. 'All will be well if you don't panic, no, don't panic.'

Stopping the car in a lane he led the way to a field. Looking at me as though I had been thrust upon him like some poltergeist he spoke quietly, 'Stand still by the gate and send them upalong.' His stick waved in the direction of Tintagel as he unlatched the gate and went out of sight with Pauline hard on his heels.

I stood in the lane telling myself that Mr Knowles's opinion of my competence was of no consequence; the important thing was that, if only for a day, I wasn't working in a bleak field. Here was a perfect spring morning, with sunshine bathing the lane and bringing out the fresh smell of the green leaves, and there was to be a nice walk ahead. Feeling full of confidence I heard the bleating sheep approach and took a couple of steps forward. They cast their eyes on me and refused to budge!

'Fool, you fool, stand back else we'll never get started.' Mr Knowles's words reached my ears before he started shouting at the sheep, 'Get on dammit, go through!' After all these months the little man had shown signs of coming to life!

Woolly bodies with red markings on their backs pushed their way through the opening and the air filled with bleats. 'How many are there for heaven's sake?' I asked.

'Forty-six. Now make haste and get ahead of them. Stay ahead of the flock and you won't lose any. I'll meet you at Tintagel soon after three o'clock. That gives you five hours.' With this, for him, torrent of words, he turned abruptly towards his car, evidently not wishing to see the difficulty I had in weaving through the sheep to get ahead and act as leader.

Boldly I walked in front trying to catch odd pieces of conversation from Pauline at the rear of the flock who was darting from left to right picking wild flowers. I soon found myself moving from side to side to prevent the sheep overtaking me!

'Let's change places, Pauline,' I suggested, then added with irony, 'You're more proficient than I am. I don't even know where I'm going.' She didn't rise to my flattery and wasn't concerned at the possibility of being led astray.

'Keep going, Pat. There's a little village ahead, my task will be as great as yours then, you'll see.'

A small row of cottages came into sight. As I passed them I idly wondered what saint's name had been used to honour this little hamlet. A sudden bark, the unexpected appearance of a dog coming towards us and my thoughts quickly turned from saints to flocks! Without warning, four sheep jumped over a garden wall and immediately set to work eating the neat flower beds! I couldn't leave my position as leader, neither could Pauline come up from the rear. Panic? no, not yet, someone would surely see our predicament and help. Someone did.

'My dear life, get they sheep out at once,' shouted a

woman wearing a flowered apron. 'My dear life, they be eating the last of me daffs.'

'We can't do anything. We daren't leave the others,' I cried turning to Pauline for corroboration. She stood immobilized too!

'Jack!' the owner of the daffs screamed, 'Jack, make 'aste 'ere.' Jack loomed large in the doorway of the cottage not realizing what he had to make 'aste for. He looked straight to the road taking in the flock of sheep and two land girls. A glimmer of a smile touched his lips before the woman pushed him from the doorway into the garden. 'There! Take 'and to they lot avore me garden's scat to pieces. Make 'aste I tell 'ee.'

Jack ran into the cottage and reappeared with a thick gnarled stick. Brandishing the stick close to the sheep he said in a soft voice, 'Shoo! Shoo! Get out the way you came, me 'ansomes.' As if the sheep understood Jack's soft words, they calmly jumped back into the road leaving behind a devastation of stems and flowers and an irate woman looking to where her last daffs had been. 'Tis your fault,' she scowled at Jack. 'Never did care over me garden, did you? Me daffs made no odds either.'

We left the village and Jack at the mercy of the lover of daffodils. On we went with Pauline still intent on gathering wild flowers but keeping her eyes open for any unusual movements among the flock. At last! A wooden signpost painted with the magical words,

Tintagel, 2 miles. Not far now – but how and when were we to stop and eat our lunch?

'There's no alternative, we'll simply have to eat while walking along,' Pauline said, taking her pasty from her tin box with ease. I found myself trying to juggle with tin box, food and a thick stick I had picked up along the way. In exasperation I threw the food away and unsuccessfully tried to light a cigarette. But this didn't really matter, for I was proud that we'd been entrusted, without any experience, with a flock of forty-six. Feeling pleased with myself and my WLA life, I relaxed: 'There's a new film at the cinema—' The words were hardly out of my mouth when the bleating started and about a dozen sheep vanished through a gap on our right.

'Oh, why on earth didn't you see the opening, Pat?' Pauline asked crossly.

'And if I had seen it how would you have stopped them?' I retaliated. 'Anyway, It's no good arguing, go after them Pauline while I watch these in the road. I'm the leader, aren't I?' Pauline went through the wide gap and the rest of the sheep followed her! I wasn't serving any useful purpose standing in the road alone so why not join them?

'Heavens!' I exclaimed, 'it's a coal yard!'

'Thanks for stating the obvious. Just tell me how we get them out of here.'

I stood and watched the sheep clambering the

mounds of coal in their fright – or was it inquisitiveness to see what was over the other side?

'They're getting dirty, Pauline.' My remark caused even more irritation. As Pauline turned on me in anger, she slipped. Her body slithered to the ground amongst the coal.

'They are dirty, I'm dirty. It's your turn now, Little Bo Peep!' Knee-deep in coal, up I went. 'Shoo! Shoo! Get out the way you came.' After all, these magical words had worked for Jack! Alas! they looked stupidly from me to Pauline.

'You silly beasts,' I shouted in temper and waved my arms in desperation. There was no reaction, just continual bleats of 'Baa! Baa! Baa!' and looks devoid of interest.

I spent nearly half an hour taking orders from Pauline, doing this, doing that, going this way and going that way. We threw large lumps of coal at the woolly bodies but this only seemed to emphasise their immovability. I began to think that these stupid animals were going to get the better of us and if they did, what then? Would Mr Knowles find us? 'Don't panic' he'd said.

'Let's sit and have a cigarette, Pauline,' I suggested as I scrambled down between sheep and coal, 'No need to panic.'

'Panic? I've got an uncontrollable desire to leave them here.'

'Maybe a car or a lorry will pass,' I said half-heartedly.

''Aven't got a car or a lorry, will a bike do?' The voice came from behind. We turned with relief and saw a ruddy-faced man holding a bicycle and looking decidedly amused.

'I 'eard shouting so came to see what's on,' he laughed. 'Where you taking 'em to?'

'Tintagel, and it looks as if they are objecting to the walk.'

'Hold 'ard, maids. One of 'ee come out on the road and stop 'em going back to Camelford. You,' his eyes looked me up and down, 'look like a smithy so a while longer in the yard will make no odds to 'ee. When I start to coose 'em, raise your voice then 'op it through the gap ahead of 'em. Soon 'ave 'em out, maids.'

With the help of this good Samaritan we extricated the sheep from coal and yard, and we were once again on our way, now realizing that two ignorant girls were not enough to manage a flock of forty-six sheep. However, Tintagel could not be far, nothing much could happen now.

As we approached a road junction a convoy of American trucks loomed towards us from the left, headed by a motor bike. Bike and trucks stopped. I paused with arms and stick stretched wide, and silently prayed that the sheep would cease moving until the American vehicles continued on their way. Glancing behind me I could see the sheep were half turning, evidently looking for another means of escape! After listening to jeers and laughter coming from the trucks followed by offers of a lift, we lost our tempers.

'Blast you and your help!' Pauline's voice rang above the confused noise of soldiers and sheep. 'How long do you think we can stand here like this? For God's sake, move on.'

'Preferably all the way to the United States,' I added with sarcasm, but taunts from Pauline and me only brought even wider grins and snappier replies. The despatch rider turned from the front of the convoy and rode slowly towards us. What was he up to now? Don't panic, I reminded myself. I stepped backwards away from the pathway of the motor bike only to fall on a woolly body and be carried on to the ground with bleats of 'Baa Baa! Baa!' piercing my ears.

Feeling hot and dirty I scrambled to my feet swearing under my breath, humiliated that I had been floored by a timid beast! Gathering my wits and what remaining dignity I had, I bent to retrieve my food box and once again I was grovelling amongst ovine hooves. 'Gee, honey, we're sorry,' only infuriated me more.

'When we've moved on how you gonna get them over the crossroads, honey?' asked the rider, now showing some concern. How indeed? An open road to the right and left meant that it was anyone's guess as to what would happen if we were left on our own to cope. I looked back at Pauline and could see the uncertainty on her face, Our confidence had faded, we were

114

both visualizing the possible chaos without help, help from dozens of jeering Yanks.

'Before you move on, would you block the road to left and right?' my voice was full of iciness at having to concede defeat.

'Sure, honey,' the fair-haired soldier smiled and promptly stopped his engine. Wheeling the bike over to the trucks he bellowed, 'Okay fellers, everyone out. Advance and form guard of honour to sheep and shepherdesses. Move it, fellers.' The loud stamping of army boots and the onrush of men only served to agitate the flock even more. They jostled together before turning their backs on me, determined to outflank Pauline. The two ranks of soldiers left the road clear and I walked ahead . . . alone. I was a leader but nothing was following me! As I watched Pauline rushing to and fro I couldn't resist recalling Mr Knowles's words of wisdom, 'Don't panic, no, don't panic.' Then we heard the tinkling of a bicycle bell and the ruddy-faced man last seen at the coal yard came peddling up behind Pauline.

'God Almighty! With a damn Yankee army you're still struggling with the beasts. Thoft I'd follow 'ee, takes a Cornishman to coose these beggars from the roads.' The good Samaritan on two wheels vigorously kept his hand on his bicycle bell at the same time lifting and pushing the front wheel into the sheep. Again they hustled against one another until their bodies reversed. They came scurrying across the road towards me with bike and bell on their tails and I caught a glimpse of rows of arms raised in salute as Pauline and the Cornish- man passed the Americans.

'You won't come to no more 'arm, maids, so I'll go backalong.'

When the man had pedalled away Pauline became her usual calm self again. 'That surely must be the last hurdle, Pat. Look, there's Brown Willy so we can't be far away now.'

I glanced at the hills to be seen in the distance but I had lost all interest in the surrounding countryside and the sheep. I was hot, dirty and bruised and my feet and legs ached.

I was taking off my heavy green jumper when Pauline let out a piercing shriek which made me stand rigid with apprehension. With my jumper half over my head I waited to hear what great sudden disaster was about to happen, or had happened!

'Pat, look out, they are going to jump the hedge. Oh hell!'

It was too late to stop this catastrophe for already half the flock had disappeared into a field and the rest were clambering up the hedge in quick pursuit. Peering over the hedge our hearts sank even further when we saw another flock in the same field. There was nothing to do but watch the sheep mix together!

'What the devil do we do now?' asked Pauline pensively.

'Who cares?' I answered. 'There must be at least a hundred there and we can't tell the difference between them.' This was the last straw, I sat down and burst into tears!

'Come now, Pat,' Pauline attempted to cheer me, 'I'll go along to that large grey house and see if I can find a farmer who will help us. "Don't panic, no, don't panic," I'll find someone.'

I sat down again and lit a cigarette. As far as I was concerned she could find General Montgomery! To hell with sheep! I lay back looking at the cloudless blue sky and wondered how shepherds managed in these wild parts of Cornwall. My silent question was answered. I heard a whistle and the call 'Shep'. Sitting up I watched the miraculous parting of the two flocks, Within ten minutes this wonderful dog called Shep had obeyed the whistles of his master and our forty-six sheep stood by the hedge which they had jumped over.

'All is well,' said Pauline, 'we've only got to get them in the road once more.'

'Tis easier said than done,' the farmer told us sternly. 'You two take your places as leader and driver and Shep will do the rest. I want you all safely off my premises and quick.'

At last we reached Tintagel, but where was the field that these unfortunate sheep were to graze in until they dropped their lambs? They too, surely, must be pleased the journey was over?

With a sigh of relief we saw Mr Knowles leaning against his car, obviously more interested in the time than our arrival. 'It's half past four, had any trouble?' he mumbled.

Pauline and I burst into laughter at this obtuse remark. 'Trouble? It's been like a journey into the unknown,' I said. 'Don't ever ask me to take part in such a thing again.'

Slumped in the back of the car, I listened while Pauline kept up a one-sided conversation telling the little man of our experiences during the last six hours and the hazards of competing with low walls, flower beds, open gaps, coal yards, convoys of trucks and low hedges. 'We didn't panic at all and there was a good Samaritan who followed us for miles,' she informed him.

I looked at Mr Knowles's profile, there was a twitching at the corner of his mouth. I glanced at the driver's mirror and could see his eyes, his first smile since we'd come to Wadebridge!

Chapter 10

Bluebell Picking

TWO days later we were surprised to find the lorry already standing waiting for us. Why was Roy so early this morning? On closer inspection we realized it was a different lorry. The girls in the truck jerked their thumbs towards the cab: 'A different driver, too. Roy's sick,' they said. Walking towards the lorry, Nell and Jackie quickly spotted a new occupant. They made straight for the cab door demanding to know where Roy and Cecil were.

'My name is Harry. You're having a different foreman too. From what I 'ear tell, I wouldn't put it past Cecil to be sick, sick and fed up with you lot!' said the pleasant looking man.

'Watch it, mate, you only say things like that with a smile on your face. Anyway, where are you taking us today?' Nell asked.

'Delabole. Bill Craddock is waiting with more teddies for 'ee.'

'Okay, Harry. Just don't try any funny tricks when driving 'cos we've been flung to the back of the lorry once too often. Watch it or else!' Nell warned him before joining us.

The lorry started then came to a sudden halt. Harry jumped from his cab and came round the back with a broad grin. Boldly he asked if anyone would like to ride in the front with him. Without any hesitation Bunny was up and over the tail-end, falling into the new driver's arms as he helped her down.

'Don't worry, mates,' Nell smiled smugly. 'We're all going to get a turn, and I'll find out if the sod is married, too!'

Reaching the field at Delabole our new foreman stood waiting by an old derelict shed made of galvanize. Bill Craddock was tall, slightly built and dressed in black: black boots, black trousers and waistcoat, black jacket and an old black trilby.

'All we need now are a few black looks from him and he'll be bloody perfect,' cracked Jackie in a sullen voice. This brought a burst of laughter from the gang and a scowl from the dark-clad figure. Indeed, he looked like a prophet of doom. His face clouded even more with ill-humour when Nell greeted him with her usual cockney salutation. 'Wotcha cock! We've come to 'elp yer but let's 'ave a fag first.' She thrust a packet of cigarettes towards him in a friendly gesture but he ignored the act.

'Come to 'elp *me*? By God, you're an army come to 'elp the war!'

'Look, Bill, we don't care who helps who,' Peggy butted in. 'I must tell you first that we don't work in the rain and secondly we go over the hedge when we want to. Understand?'

Whether Bill understood what Peggy alluded to regarding the hedge we couldn't tell for he ignored her too, his attention riveted on Bunny who was again renewing her make-up. She slowly put her compact and lipstick in her pocket and smiled straight at Bill, revealing her lovely teeth and dimples. It didn't impress him, he simply glanced at Harry with a stony face. 'Be on your way, son, and mind the time you come back.'

'Make it early if it rains, Harry,' called Kay gaily after him.

'Make 'aste and get to work. You're here to pick up the teddies and that's what you'll do for I'll not stand any nonsense from you. Rows are marked and Jimmy's waiting,' Bill said sourly. Jimmy Coombes sat on the tractor with half a smile on his face, no doubt he'd had plenty of time to relate his version of the way we worked at Tintagel! However, maybe Bill had a hidden sense of humour and his gruffness was only a facade because he was confronted with eighteen strange females?

After an hour's work we once again started moving the sack markers to our advantage and Bill was at the end of our deceit. As we didn't trust Jimmy Coombes we waited for the tractor to slowly pass each couple and then quickly dragged the bundles into the new position. In spite of the fact that he kept an eagle eye on us, Bill didn't notice what had happened, he merely carried on picking up more potatoes at the end of the rows, grumbling to himself that he couldn't work any faster!

'What's the time, Bill?' Fanny called to him.

Every back straightened hoping to see another long uncovering act. We were disappointed. Bill put his hand quickly under his black jacket and pulled on a chain and his watch fell into his hand from a small pocket. Looking disdainfully at the few rows that had been dug he mumbled 'Crib time' and started to walk towards the galvanized shack. We followed, smiling to ourselves. A few yards on he suddenly stopped, turned and surveyed the rows from top to bottom. Without a word he went into the shed, picked up an old black shoulder bag, sat on a rusty oil drum and began to eat.

'Want a fish-paste sandwich, Bill?' Nell's second gesture of friendship was refused. She shrugged her shoulders. 'Please your bloody self, you miserable sod. The seagulls will like 'em.'

'What the hell's the matter with him?' asked Jackie turning away from Bill and the oil drum.

'It's just possible that he has lost someone,' Pauline whispered. 'Give him time, we'll make him smile.'

'But he isn't looking sad,' I said, 'just bad tempered.'

We had lit our cigarettes and only taken a couple of

puffs when the figure in black jumped up unexpectedly off the drum.

'Ten minutes is gone, that's all you be getting. First you'll move all they sacks back to where I put them and you'll now be getting longer pieces for your trouble. I was 'elping you lot but you're so puffed up with your townie smoke you didn't see!' For the rest of the day Bill Craddock spent his time walking slowly up and down the rows. When we started a relay to and from the hedge he ordered the remaining girls not to idle and pick up the potatoes from the temporary empty gap.

The only girl to whom he showed any signs of leniency was Pauline. Every now and then he would hover near her and when her bucket was full of potatoes he stepped forward quickly and held the sack open for her. A piece of their conversation drifted over to Kay and me who were nearby. 'Yes, I do like ballet,' Bill was informing Pauline, 'and opera. I listen to it for hours.' Bill's sombre face had lightened for a few minutes as he spoke of his two loves.

Kay and I smiled at each other. This could be a break-through. I casually walked the few yards to where Nell and Jackie were bent double, engrossed in conversation as they absently threw potatoes into their buckets. Bending over I said, 'Hey! Bill likes ballet and opera so why . . .' I wasn't allowed to finish. The two girls looked up at me with scorn.

'So what!' Jackie exclaimed, 'I like jitterbugging and jazz.'

'And what do you want me to do?' asked Nell, 'A bleedin' dance on my toes around 'im for another peace offering?'

'Just pass the news down the row. Surely we must all know some little bit of opera. Tell the girls to sing anything they know.'

'Let us start with *Madam Butterfly*. Do you know "One Fine Day"?' I asked Kay. She took a deep breath and raised her voice high.

'One fine day I'll meet him, along the blue horizon . . .'

Bill's steps slowly faltered as he passed the assumed soprano. Hesitating for a few seconds only, he walked back to Kay. 'You like opera too?' he asked with interest.

'Oh yes, very much. Pat likes it too, don't you?' she smiled.

'Then it's a pity you don't sing the right bloody words!'

'They call me Mimi . . .' I started to sing, hoping to pique his curiosity. Both black eyebrows shot up as he fired his question.

'What opera is that from?'

'*La Bohème*,' I answered, hoping I'd got my music right.

Deep in thought he went on a few yards before

stopping to listen to Nell. 'O My Beloved Father . . .' she began deliberately.

'Get the bloody tune right, maid,' he told her quietly without any trace of resentment. In fact his lips began to smile when the next couple, Jimmy and Peggy, took up their cue by singing something from *The Barber of Seville* in loud, clear voices. We stood watching Bill carry on to the end of the row where Bunny and Grace were working. What aria had they in mind? Amused, we saw Bunny turn her bucket upside down and balance on it. Clear and loud, her serious tones echoed into the air.

'O Romeo, Romeo! Wherefore art thou Romeo?'

'By God, that's a bit of Shakespeare. Do 'ee know any more?' Bill pushed back his old trilby for the first time. Thin whisps of black hair lay in all directions on his head but he was completely unaware of his appearance as he looked eagerly at Bunny.

'Countryman! Land girls!' Bunny mocked, 'lend me your ears.'

'O pardon me, thou bleedin' piece of earth,' cried Sue.

Bill swung around, he wasn't sure who had quoted this sentence so bellowed to us all: 'It's "thou bloody piece of earth"' he claimed, standing with straight back and firm lips.

'No it isn't,' Sue maintained. 'It's "bleedin' earth", I'm sure.'

Bill Craddock began to walk towards Sue, determined

to change her mind. The rest of us had spotted the lorry and turned our backs on both of them, but the argument continued as they slowly followed. Nell was quickly walking ahead of us. Turning her head she said, 'At last the bugger has something to say, girls!' She moved swiftly to the front of the lorry and held onto the passenger door. Looking straight at Bunny who had also edged up closely behind her, Nell yelled across to Sue, 'It's your turn to co-pilot. Hurry up and leave 'im to 'is swearing.'

Bunny, looking somewhat piqued, moved to the back of the lorry and clambered in. 'Thought it was my turn today,' she smirked.

'Mate,' replied Nell, climbing in behind her, 'do you realize every time we get in this lorry it's a separate journey and we're lucky to reach the end of each one safely? Anyway, you're safer back 'ere with us till we know more about the driver!'

As we moved off, Bill stood kicking the ground with his boot.

'See you tomorrow,' Jackie called to him, 'See both you and your soddin' earth.' This remark caused our new foreman to turn away and kick into the ground even harder with his other foot!

As the days passed in Bill Craddock's company, we began to learn from him interesting facts about the north of Cornwall. He sat on his oil drum telling us about folklore, indeed, he seemed to be a fount of knowledge on most subjects and it became a pleasure to sit and listen. Even if we were not concerned or curious about all his information, nobody interrupted, for while he talked he forgot about time and work, which suited us fine. When asked by Pauline how he came by all his knowledge he simply smiled and stated, 'I've been a tramp most of me life.' A tramp? Alone on the roads for days, for weeks or months. No wonder he was intolerant of working with people, let alone a gang of girls from city life who were out to dodge work and have fun doing so! But by our evasion, ridicule and arguments, Bill had begun to mellow, or so we thought.

One day while we were working in a field at Boscastle, unrest crept through our gang again. Once more we were well and truly bored with the seemingly never-ending chore of potato picking. After eating our lunch quickly and listening to Bill's description of the nearby Valency valley, eight of us decided to explore it for ourselves. With a stern warning from Bill to 'Make 'aste' we almost ran down the sloping fields towards the stream that ran from the Bodmin Moors and twisted seaward. Over the other side of the stream lay a carpet of bluebells. Determined to pick some for our parents we searched the bank looking for a low point where we could wade across the stream in our wellingtons.

'Stepping stones here,' called Kay. Joining hands to help our balance we were soon over. After gazing at the lovely expanse of these blue wild flowers we bent down and gathered armfuls. What a contrast to dirty buckets of potatoes! Bearing in mind Bill's request for haste we returned to the stepping stones, our arms laden. Too late we realized the importance of keeping at least one arm free in order to help balance each other.

'Now how the hell do we get back,' Jackie wailed.

'Don't panic, the stream must be shallow at some point,' I said.

Kay and I set off to the right while the other girls went to the left, leaving Jackie to drop her flowers and smoke. Five minutes later Kay and I had successfully waded slowly through the water and were safely on the bank, calling to the others to follow. We watched as they slowly and carefully made their way to us, with the exception of Jackie who stood bemoaning the fact that that she was small and her wellingtons were short too!

'I'm going back over the stepping stones, someone help me,' she pleaded. 'I don't want the bleedin' flowers, just help me.'

Falling in with her wishes, back we went to the stones and formed a chain of hands to reach her. Throwing half her bluebells down she groped and grabbed the nearest hand. Deciding she was now safe she held tightly on to the remaining flowers.

Then halfway across the stream her foot slipped and she tumbled backwards into the water, her bluebells falling in all directions. Soaking wet, she dragged herself up holding fast to the stones for support. Standing knee deep in the stream she realized that it was now easier and less frightening to carry on walking without help. As soon as she had floundered safely to the bank we burst out laughing, at the same time pulling her wellingtons off. Her socks were dragged off her feet and the water squeezed out. 'Bloody hell, my fags are wet,' she gasped. 'Sod it all.'

'Don't worry about cigarettes,' I said, 'we all have some. Let's get back to the field. Bill will understand, I'm sure.' I wasn't at all sure! Although his manner appeared to have softened during the midday conversations, resentment was all too plain when he was forced to watch the receding backs of girls as they made their way to the hedge. His familiar sullen face would survey what filled sacks there were and with dissatisfaction he would grumble to himself, 'By God, another hour of the war gone for nothing.' How would he react when he saw the bedraggled Jackie?

Lighting another cigarette from the butt of the one she had quickly smoked, Jackie looked at us aghast. 'What? Me go back to work in these wet clothes? Not bloody likely. I'm getting home somehow, and if you lot have got any sense you will too!' We looked at each other and were hit simultaneously with an idea. Why not all get wet? Why not all go home? Bill would understand a simple accident and show compassion towards us. Taking off our wellingtons and socks we waded in the river up to our knees, dampened our jumpers and hair, then slowly trailed back to the field. Smothering our giggles and trying to look sorry for ourselves we faced inquisitive stares from the other girls and a nasty, glowering, fixed gaze from Bill.

'Fell in the river,' said Jackie truthfully. She moved her boots up and down and we could hear the squelching noise of feet and water. From the end of her hair droplets of water fell onto her shoulders. It was obvious Bill believed her but mistrust was apparent when he cast his eyes over the rest of us.

'Oh? I s'pose you lot fell in too? Likely story!' he sneered. 'The stream isn't that deep, so don't try and fox me, maids.'

'We were clinging to each other and—' I began, but Bill cut in: 'And now your clothes are clinging to you. Don't worry, the sun's about to shine, that'll 'elp dry you cos I can't do a damn thing about it.' He turned away with a half-smile.

'We're doing something about it, we're going home,' Kay said.

The dark figure twisted around angrily, 'You'll 'ave a long walk. Makes no odds to me that you'll not make it.' Again he turned from us with the semblance of a weak smile. At that moment we heard a faint whistle in the distance. A train! Without any more hesitation we picked up our food boxes and walked from the field, feeling very uncomfortable in our wet clothes.

'You'll not be getting away with this, by God, you won't.' Refusing to listen to the warning note in Bill Craddock's voice, eight undesirable-looking girls started trekking towards Camelford station. It was to be quite a walk and the sun began to shine. A breeze blew pleasantly and we felt quite happy until we realized the effect this weather was having on our clothes. We were drying, and drying too quickly! There would be no evidence of our so-called mishap by the time we reached Wadebridge and Mr Knowles wouldn't swallow our story when we reported to him!

When we arrived at the station, we found we had nearly an hour's wait for the next train. Assuring the sleepy porter that we would pay our fare into Wadebridge station the following day we sat on a seat wishing it would rain, anything to keep our clothes damp. Kay nudged me and nodded towards some red fire buckets. Slowly rising from the seat we casually made our way over to them. 'Water! Shall we?' whispered Kay with some excitement.

'May as well, we've nothing to lose,' I answered.

'Leave me out of it,' said Jackie shivering, 'I'm still bleedin' soaking but I'll watch the porter doesn't see you.' She walked through the same door that the porter had entered. Hearing some conversation in progress we hastily lifted the buckets and emptied the contents over each other! Ten minutes later we were on the train huddled in a compartment together, all shivering.

When we arrived at Wadebridge we began to feel a little apprehensive. Clutching our limp and fading bluebells we reached the bridge and were even more crestfallen when the lorry appeared with the rest of the gang! It had taken us all afternoon to get home and the soaking had achieved nothing, except a future report from Bill!

'So what! I've had enough of the Land Army anyway,' Jackie sniffed.

Chapter 11

The Chest Parade

THE following morning I woke with a nasty cold and lay in bed watching Kay get ready for work. I didn't relish staying home on my own but my head ached badly and I felt so cold.

'I've a good mind to stay home too,' said Kay as she reluctantly put on her working dungarees.

'Wait until tomorrow, I'll feel better and then we can both walk around town,' I told her encouragingly. 'After yesterday's activities I may not be the only one to stay in bed.'

When Kay had left, Mrs Gill brought a cup of tea and aspirins to me. 'Just you stay there, my dear,' she said. 'It's all that Craddock's fault. Fancy making you find your own way home.'

'But Mrs Gill, it was our own fault, we wanted the bluebells. When Jackie fell it gave us . . .'

'Yes, my dear, it must have given you quite a fright. Thinking of your parents too. Never mind, go to sleep again, don't worry.' I snuggled into the bedclothes and smiled. Had that sleepy porter at Camelford discovered the empty buckets and if so what had he thought about the sudden disappearance of gallons of water?

During the afternoon I got up and dressed in civvies intending to take a stroll by the river and go to the station to pay the debt that Kay and I owed. My eye caught the half-filled bottle of 'Evening In Paris' perfume. Kay had said, 'Use it when you like, but do use it sparingly.' I picked up the bottle and unscrewed the top when there was a sudden knock on the door and Mrs Gill's voice asking if I was all right. In my haste to open the door I dropped the small blue phial onto the dressing table, spilling the rest of the sweet-smelling liquid.

'Oh heavens!' I spoke aloud in my panic. 'What will Kay say? How will I tell her?' I was sure of one thing, and that was that she would lose her temper! The bedroom reeked of the stuff as I put my coat on and headed for the town wondering if the local chemist sold any perfume nearly as nice. I hurried over the bridge and was a few yards away from the chemist's shop when I came face to face with Mr Knowles. He barred my way with the help of his stick. 'Where are you going? Why aren't you at work?'

'I have a nasty cold and I'm going to buy some perfume. Oh yes, and I need aspirins too,' I told him, then quickly pushed past him and fled into the chemist's knowing that he would wait for my reappearance.

'No, we only sell lavender water,' the assistant replied to my query.

'That won't do,' I told her dismally. 'I'll have some aspirins instead.'

'Instead? Aren't you feeling well?' the woman eyed me dubiously.

'I'm fine. My friend will be needing them now that I can't replace her favourite perfume. She's bound to break out in a sweat when she gets home!' Holding the aspirins in my hand I went out to the street to see Mr Knowles standing talking to Jackie. I stepped up to both waving the tablets at Jackie.

'Take two immediately. You should never have got out of your bed, let alone walk all this way for medication. She really is looking ill, isn't she, Mr Knowles?'

'Seems you are both looking rather odd at this moment,' he said.

I tugged on Jackie's arm and led her around the corner and on to the station. 'What did he have to say to you,' I asked.

'Nothing! As usual, nothing. I'd only just bumped into him.'

'Well, at least he now knows that we aren't dodging work.'

'I don't care what the 'ell 'e thinks. After our next leave I'm resigning. Only a couple of months to go, anyway.'

We walked back alongside the Egloshayle river and I

sat on the bank waiting for Kay to return. It wasn't long before the lorry stopped and Kay jumped down. She was looking quite happy.

'Guess what, Pat,' she enthused, 'we land girls are going to take part in a parade through the town along with other forces and we will march to the American band. Should be fun.'

'Yes. When is this to be?' I had caught her enthusiasm and I also hoped this would reduce her anger about the perfume.

'This coming Sunday afternoon,' she smiled. Dropping her food box in the hall as usual, she mounted the stairs and I followed slowly, feeling a mixture of pleasure and apprehension. The aroma had permeated from the bedroom and was now lingering in the air of the stairway. Kay reached the bathroom door and hesitated. Sniffing the air she turned to me swiftly, suspicion wiping the delight from her face. 'What can I smell?'

'Your perfume, Kay. It was an accident, I'm sorry.'

Without waiting for any further explanation from me, Kay ran up the next short flight of stairs and pushed the bedroom door open. Grabbing the blue bottle she held it up to the light, then faced me again as I stood in the doorway watching her temper rise. 'You spilled it on purpose,' she accused, throwing the empty bottle on the dressing table.

We stared at each other, my anger now rising to match hers. 'Let me explain,' I said. Dishevelled from her day's work she sat on the edge of the bed and listened. When I told her of the encounter of Jackie and Mr Knowles all traces of temper left her face and she smiled once more.

'Sorry, Pat,' she said, then added with a reproving glance, 'don't think I shall forget this in a hurry.' The short, unpleasant incident passed and our minds were filled with the coming Sunday and the parade.

The day dawned bright and sunny, and we spent the morning giving our uniforms an extra brushing. At 1 o'clock we were gathered in a field along with groups from various other forces. Confusion seemed to abound regarding who should walk where, the only certainty being that the Americans would be first in line following their own band. Eventually the RAF were shuffled into position behind them, then a small contingent of the British Army followed. On their heels were the Fleet Air Arm backed up by the Wrens. We watched as the official looked with hesitation from the Home Guard to us. Giving him no more time to decide who was to be next in place of rank Nell stepped forward. 'Where the 'ell do you think you are putting us, mate?' she asked indignantly, 'we are one of the bloody Forces, you know.' The harassed official wiped his brow in the heat of the sun.

'Well,' he said, 'we have the Boy Scouts and the Girl Guides and I thought maybe you land girls could bring up the rear.' Confusion turned to uproar as the whole gang began to protest.

'You think wrong, mate,' Nell told him. 'Come on, girls, we ain't gonna march at the back of that lot!'

We began to walk from the field declaring that land girls had been publicly insulted. The official strode quickly after us. 'Girls, listen to me, please. It is just as important to bring up the rear as to march in front,' he cajoled.

'Is that so?' Kay's temper began to rise. 'If it's important to be at the back then why aren't the bloody Wrens here?'

While the argument had been taking place all eyes were watching. Laughter had broken out from different sections and even the Boy Scouts and Girl Guides were giggling. We took off our hats and walked another couple of yards away when the flustered official overtook us. Once again he tried to soothe our anger. Loosening his tie he started bargaining. 'Now, when the service is over you can be the first in line behind the band. How's that?'

'That's all right,' said Jimmy, 'the Yanks are only visitors anyway. Remember, we do more work than all those lined up.'

On went our hats again and when we lined across in fours, I found myself between Pauline and Kay. Something looked amiss. It was Pauline's bare head. 'Where's your hat?' I asked her.

'Oh, I lost it weeks ago and sent for another. Instead of replacing a hat they substituted a pair of shoes that fitted my father perfectly! He's thrilled to bits and I don't want a hat anyway. Think of the clothing coupons he saved!'

The band started to play and eventually our paces became regular. Over the level-crossing and onto the bridge we marched. Halfway over the bridge Kay and I suddenly looked at each other, voicing the same words. 'What the devil was that?' Simultaneously we put our hands up to our hats. A flock of seagulls had swooped over and their droppings had fallen on our hats and shoes!

'This wouldn't have happened to us if we weren't at the back. Bloody Wrens,' Kay hissed, 'they never get dirty!'

When we reached the playing field where the service was to be held, the heat was terrific. The sun seemed to burn through our thick green jumpers making us feel very weary and weak. In a short while one American fainted, then another went down.

'Stay on your legs, girls. Show 'em we are tougher than them.' This was an order from Nell, 'Don't one of you dare fall!'

When the service ended Nell promptly left us and made straight for the official. The two walked swiftly over to an American lieutenant and gestured in our direction. All three beckoned us to join them. Happily we ignored the other contingents and shuffled our way between the Americans and their band. The Lieutenant smiled broadly and his voice boomed across the field. 'Okay, girls,' he said, 'we'll have the chest parade in front as they should be!'

Chapter 12

Bunny's Catastrophe

O N Saturday afternoons we either went to Bodmin on shopping sprees, when money and clothing coupons would allow, or we watched the Americans play a ball game in the playing field along Egloshayle road. Occasionally we would go to church on Sunday mornings and it was on one Sabbath morning that Kay and I witnessed our glamour girl's disaster. We had called at Pauline's billet and waited in the front room while she and Phyllis got ready to go to church. Suddenly, there was a frantic knocking on the front door. The landlady, Mrs Hornbrook, hurried through the passage, calling to her husband, 'Whoever can it be, Reg?' She opened the door and her startled words reached us. 'Who are you? Do I know you?'

A distraught voice answered. 'Oh! Of course you do! I'm Bunny, please, please help me.' Mrs Hornbook, now assured that this wasn't some kind of hoax, ushered Bunny into the room and kept her arm around the sobbing girl. We stared: Bunny was clutching a brown-stained towel tightly rolled round her head. Pauline and Phyllis rushed into the room followed by Reg. It was some time before the tears subsided and Bunny became coherent. Slowly she loosened the towel.

'I was in the middle of dyeing my hair and look what has happened, it's gone all colours and is bloody well falling out!' she cried. Pauline removed the towel completely from her head and we stood open-mouthed. Her normally pretty blonde hair was streaked a nasty mauve-brown colour. Indeed, she had cause for alarm, for her hair was also falling out in handfuls. Seeing the mixture of both amusement and dismay on our faces Bunny grabbed the towel to her head again, 'Oh God, what do I look like?' she wailed.

'You look like the Wreck of the *Hesperides*, dear,' Pauline said, 'but never mind, let's go up to the bathroom and see what we can do.' They disappeared for half an hour and when they came back into the room Bunny seemed a little calmer. Surveying the damage, five pairs of hands scoured Bunny's scalp. There was a definite greenish tinge about the roots and the end strands resembled steel wool! Mrs Hornbrook stood by, bewilderment on her face, while Reg, who was a jovial Dan, and always had a ready laugh whether it was for or against the gang, drew back, smiling as he began to roll a cigarette.

'You maids always be up to something, dammit,' he

said. 'Now you've really come a cropper, maid, sure enough.'

These words brought a fresh flood of tears from Bunny, causing her mascara to run in streaks down her cheeks. Her face was devoid of lipstick and rouge, making her look terribly pale. Once again Pauline remained calm and took the situation in hand.

'We'll find a hairdresser straight away,' she said optimistically.

'But it's Sunday! Besides, I don't want anyone else to see me like this. Oh! what a mess, I won't be able to go out for ages.'

'Who cares what day it is, we'll find someone who will do something about your mess,' Pauline told her firmly.

Going to church was forgotten as the five of us shambled down Egloshayle road taking care that Bunny was surrounded in the middle of our small circle. Those who did catch a glimpse of a turban-towelled girl on this Sunday morning must have thought she was crazy and that her companions were joining in the spring madness! Bunny lowered her head even further into her shoulders and kept her eyes to the ground when we came to the hairdresser's. The bell seemed to echo even louder through the shop on this quiet Sunday morning and we stood praying that someone would open the door and help. Pauline was about to press the bell once more when we saw movement. The door opened but a

few inches and a woman showed only her face, a face
that clouded with suspicion when she saw the confused
huddle of five agitated land girls.

'What do you want?' she blinked as she eyed each of
us in turn.

'Please help me,' pleaded Bunny, 'my hair is falling
out!'

'Is this some kind of joke?' the woman asked severely.
Resisting the temptation to pull the towel from Bunny's
head we pushed the forlorn girl close to the door and
stepped back still trying to conceal her. Bunny eased the
towel from her head for a few seconds then quickly
replaced it, looking gingerly around.

'Oh dear! My dear life, what have you done? Come
in quick.' The woman grabbed Bunny, Pauline followed and the door was slammed in our faces. There
was nothing to be done now but walk slowly back to
Mrs Hornbrook and wait for their return. Passing Mr
Knowles's house our eyes went automatically to his
window. There he stood, his face close to the window
pane, scratching his head. Had he seen five girls huddled
together in confusion pass by a little earlier and now
wondered where the other two were? Smiling at our
conjectures we were then faced with the oncoming Mr
Gill and his dog. The look on his face told us he knew
something, yet wanted to know more. He stood deliberately in our pathway. 'One of the maids 'ad an accident?' he asked.

'Good heavens, no. Why do you ask that?' smiled Kay.

'Tis about that a maid's gone doctors with a bandage round 'er.'

So this was the Cornish tom-tom service at full speed, was it?

'It was only a towel, Mr Gill,' I said, 'a mere accessory.'

Stepping into the road we passed him and hurried to Mrs Hornbrook who was as anxious as ourselves about the mishap. It was to be more than an hour before Pauline came in on her own.

'She's fine,' Pauline announced. 'At least her hair is all one colour now. A course of treatment will soon put this calamity right. We'll soon have our glamorous blonde back none the worse for her experience but a lot wiser. Bunny swears she'll stick to the peroxide bottle in future!'

The following day found us at St Breock where Bill Craddock awaited with his accustomed sardonic smile. He assured us that the week wouldn't be out before the damn teddies be finished. 'And,' he added, 'I'll be finished with you damned lot, too!' Bunny now wore a turban scarf which she had tightly knotted in the front. She had just checked that the scarf was securely in place when a small van drove into the field.

'You've got extra help today and I want no gaming around.' Bill snapped these words out with irritation while his eyes swept over each one of the gang. Quickly he turned his back on us and walked towards the van that had stopped a few yards away. Thinking that more land girls had been found to get the potatoes lifted urgently, we had turned our backs without interest when suddenly the sound of alien voices reached our ears.

'Good God! They're bloody foreigners,' Jackie said, appalled.

'Hush your tongue, maid,' Bill growled. 'You're foreigners, too!'

We stood still, gaping at the half-dozen young men who were also looking at us with open mouths; it was apparent that they were surprised to be facing a gang of girls and if they had understood Jackie's first words, hostile girls too! 'Germans or Italians?' we mouthed in unison.

Gleaming smiles crossed their faces. 'Italiano,' they chorused.

'Prisoners of war.' whispered Pauline, 'what a shame.'

'Shame? What the 'ell you talking about?' Jackie was perplexed.

'Wotcha cocks!' Nell bawled, 'welcome to spud bashing.' Bewilderment became visible, the six Italians looked at each other, over to Bill then dubiously to Nell, and shrugged helplessly. Obviously they didn't understand Nell's cockney accent.

'The lads are here to work, not to divert your attention. So get along to the teddies,' Bill mumbled.

146

'I'm only starting a conversation with them,' Nell said angrily.

'The only thing you start is bloody trouble, girl.'

'Oh yeah? I didn't start the bloody war, mate.'

'No, but you can damn well work harder and help finish it!'

Nell and Bill faced each other in silence for a moment.

'How the 'ell can we speak to them? Want me to send up smoke signals? You're just a miserable old sod. Come on, girls, let 'im fumble 'is way through opera and ballet with them, it might keep 'is eyes off us.' Nell stormed over the earth in temper and we followed with amusement and laughter, for the Italians ignored the foreman and were close on our heels.

With resolution we paced out our own pieces of rows to be done and dumped the bundles of sacks in their places and waited for the tractor to start. Puzzled, the Italians looked at Bill.

'Bloody maids, you've left no land for these lads,' cried Bill.

'They pinched enough land where they've come from, we're keeping our own rows so you get in the next row with them and fraternize – that's if you know how!' said Jackie with scorn. Bill Craddock gathered the prisoners together and, stifling his temper, muttered something about 'mutiny' before leading them to the row alongside. Now the tractor dug up potatoes continuously as it chugged up and down but we found we had even more resting time as the tractor had to dawdle behind the six men and Bill! 'Crib' shouted Jimmy Coombes from his seat on the tractor. The Italians swiftly stood erect, one pair of boot heels clicked loudly and six arms appeared to dither in some kind of salute! A few of us beckoned to them as we walked to get our food boxes.

'Stop work.' 'Time to eat.' 'Have a drink.' All these phrases we shouted while raising our arms up and down to our mouths. At last, with beaming smiles, they understood. Quickly they marched over to their van and pulled out their army bags and sat down near us. Bill hovered for some time before he sat. Within a few seconds, Nell, with her usual aplomb, held out a sandwich to them. 'Fish paste, mate, do you like it?' she asked.

'Fish paste?' one of the Italians queried, 'You not like?'

'Like? I'm sick of the bloody stuff, it's now seagulls' food.'

'Seagull's food?' A frown crossed his brow as he took it and peered between the two slices of bread. 'Seagulls food,' he repeated again and passed it to the other Italians then delved into his bag. Selecting a chunky sandwich he offered it to Nell. 'Spam, you like spam? You eat! I eat seagulls' food!'

When we took out our cigarettes, the thought

occurred to us that they might not have any. At first Jackie held back, moaning that she couldn't spare any, then relented and pulled out a couple from her Lucky Strike packet. Pauline collected two handfuls from the gang and handed them to the Italian who had spoken. He took them gratefully and put them on the ground. Taking two crushed cigarettes from his jacket pocket he offered them to her. 'Woodbine, you smoke my Woodbine?' he said hopefully. Not wishing to offend, Pauline accepted the crushed cigarette and slid it into her pocket. Bill had sat quietly watching the bartering, his perpetual scowl beginning to disappear.

'S'pose they aren't all bad but they be buggers all the same. Now it's time to get back to work,' he said, 'rain's coming.'

Two hours later the mist started to roll across the field and we put on our macs. To our surprise we watched the Italians scamper quickly back to their van and jump in. Thinking that they were looking for their mackintoshes we carried on working. Nearly ten minutes went by yet still there were no signs of life coming from the van.

'What the bloody 'ell is going on?' more than one voice asked suspiciously; after all, work usually carried on during a mist.

'They aren't used to our English weather and it's dampening. They'll be back again as soon as it clears,' Bill said slyly.

Various protests fell from our lips but Nell's disapproval was the loudest. With a look of horror on her face and shock in her voice she leaped over the short piece of ground that separated her from Bill. 'My God! Whose bleedin' side of the war are you on, Bill Craddock? Jesus! They ain't come to England or Cornwall for convalescence! They're in with us now, mate, all the way. Get them out of the van or we'll stop work too and walk home.' In a flash Nell's opponent submitted and slouched to the van. His face was a picture of woe as he gesticulated with his arms in an effort to make the prisoners understand that they must resume work. Gradually, one by one, they emerged.

'Oh no! Am I seeing things?' Bunny asked, holding on tightly to her turban. She had been very subdued all morning and now we followed her startled stare that was riveted on the Italians.

Each dark head was hatless revealing beautiful dark wavy hair. Peering closer we were astonished to see that each head of fine wavy hair was protected by a hairnet! Realising they had our full, curious attention, they donned their hats and hurriedly marched back to their row of potatoes, bent their backs and began speaking amongst themselves in a fast flow of Italian. Hearing our continued giggles one of the prisoners straightened his back. 'No permanente,' he said firmly, 'No permanente. We dance tonight, Lunedi day.'

'That's your problem, mate,' Nell answered him.

'We ain't loony, we're just plain bloody mad to 'ave joined the WLA.'

'*Non capisco, non capisco*,' the Italian carried on.

Seeing the dark scowl Bill gave us, we spoke no more until Jimmy Coombes shouted 'Croust'. This time the Italians rose slowly, walked to the van, pulled out their army bags and joined us as we sat on the damp earth.

Conversation during the lunch break was amusing owing to the linguistic misunderstandings. With a sandwich half raised towards his mouth one of the prisoners emitted a loud sneeze and Jackie looked across to him sullenly and said sarcastically, 'Go back and spread your bloody germs in Germany.' This remark brought smiles from all and the Italian was quick to reciprocate.

'Bloody Germans in Germany? Yes, many still there.'

'What work do you do in Italy?' asked Pauline.

'I am what you call a plumb. I start the leaks in pipes.' A weak smile even crossed Bill Craddock's face at these words spoken in broken English. The only one who didn't seem to be very amused was Bunny, eating in silence.

'What's up with you, cock?' asked Nell in a teasing voice.

All eyes were on the glamour girl as she again held her turban in place, which only made more it obvious that something was wrong. The plumbing Italian spoke in bewilderment. 'You not got a face with no hair on top?' At last Bunny gave us one of her lovely smiles.

151

Chapter 13

Transfer

THE time came when the Americans had to leave, They had spent a lot of their time at Wadebridge practising the construction of bridges over various parts of the river Camel.

One day we came home from work utterly dirty and windswept to see the convoy of trucks driving along Egloshayle road in the direction of Bodmin. Loud toots came from the trucks and Americans were shouting farewell. As Kay and I stood outside our billet a truck pulled up and stopped nearby. Stoney leaned his head out of the cab window to say a quick goodbye to Kay who now realized what was happening and was almost in tears, completely unconscious of her dishevelled appearance. The inhabitants of the road rushed from their houses to see what all the commotion was about and in no time Egloshayle road seemed to be full of people, trucks and confusion. It was all over in a few minutes and we were left listening to the drone of engines in the distance. Not a word or whisper had leaked out about their sudden departure so we were taken by complete surprise. We walked slowly into the house only to be met with a triumphant Mr Gill who was happily lighting a cigarette.

'Mmm! Mmm! It be a good job, Sarah,' he said to a sorrowful looking Mrs Gill. 'The damned Yanks have left, now maybe we'll get some peace. Yes, it be a good job.'

We were feeling too deflated to answer Mr Gill's comment.

The next few days it was a rather sad gang of girls who went to work. It was now May and at last the potato crop had finished – at least for a few months until we would start all over again.

Bill Craddock had disappeared. The last time we had seen him he had slouched away from the potato field with a scowl on his face muttering that he was glad to see the back of us!

We were given yet another foreman named Leonard Best. This man had a jovial face, a friendly nature and wore a black beret like a Frenchman. To him we were one and all called 'You bugger' so it was inevitable that we retaliated and nicknamed him 'Mr Bugger'. He was picked up by the lorry every morning at St Tudy where he lived, this being en route to the outlandish places where we were to continue to work.

The War Agricultural Committee had ordered farmers to plough up some of their barren land and plant crops, particularly potatoes, in them. The land chosen for us land girls to work on was mostly on cliff tops, full of stones and rubble. The ground had not been ploughed for years.

It was now our job to clear the fields of stones and rebuild any hedges that had fallen. The task of hedging entailed lifting heavy stones and putting earth between them and we found it was harder work than 'spud bashing'. We still faced occasional mists and their damp- ness seemed to penetrate our thick macs making us feel thoroughly miserable. Once again we looked towards the range of Brown Willy and prayed for rain.

One afternoon, after trimming straggly branches from sparsely growing bushes, we heaped them in a pile ready for burning and sat down out of sight of Leonard to smoke a cigarette. Jackie had only taken one draw when she turned and exclaimed in an exasperated tone, 'Oh Christ, 'ere 'e comes again!' She always alluded to little Mr Knowles this way whenever he came out to the fields. Following her eyes, we could just see his cap above the hedge moving towards the gateway and, as always, his little dog scampered ahead. Hastily we got to our feet and busied ourselves with the branches. Leonard peered round the pile and in a low voice warned us, 'Iss, sure 'nough tis 'im so get yourselves on your feet. You buggers are forever devising ways to waste time. Get working.'

Most of us had taken a turn in being told off by

Leonard. Phyllis was caught more than once sitting down writing poetry, Bunny was told many times to leave her make-up at home and Kay and I were rebuked for stopping to write down the words of songs that we wished to learn. Pauline and Jimmy were reproved for standing still together and harmonizing hymns. As for Jackie, every time she lit a cigarette she was reminded to keep working or 'put the buggering thing out.' All these rebukes came from Leonard with firmness but also with tolerance.

Mr Knowles sidled up to Leonard and after a few words both men looked in our direction. Leonard pointed in turn to Kay, Bunny and Jackie, then began to rub his chin with his hand.

'You three buggers come over 'ere, want to 'ave a word with 'ee,' he said, not unkindly.

The three girls stepped over to the men. A mixture of curiosity and defiance flashed across their faces, indeed, the rest of us were just as puzzled as to why they were singled out. Mr Knowles lifted his cap and scratched his head, his face reddening. 'You three are being trans-ferred to a hostel at St Erth,' he told them. 'When you get home, pack your clothes and be ready for me by nine sharp tomorrow morning.'

Kay, Bunny and Jackie started to protest but Mr Knowles, giving no explanation, turned quickly and walked from the field.

'You've 'ad it at last, you buggers. Guess Bill

Craddock reported 'ee after all,' said Leonard, 'Now you'll really 'ave to work or go back to London.'

After the shock of this news there was uproar. No one could understand why those three had been chosen for a transfer; after all, each one of us had dodged work at some time and eight of us were involved in the disappearing act with bluebells and sodden clothes.

'Only us three!' cried Jackie, 'It just ain't fair. I'm complaining to the War Ag about this. Who the hell does he think he is?'

'Well, you can do that later, right now you can stop your balling and 'oll'ing and carry on working,' ordered Leonard. He was losing patience with the whole situation. 'And look at they hedges, they be nort but codged up anyhow. Bloody maids!'

Ignoring Leonard we stormed over to the hedge to talk about this sudden event that was to take place tomorrow.

'Come back 'ere you buggers,' shouted Leonard. 'Makes no odds to me what 'appens to the three buggers. I tell 'ee, I'll not stand for this. I'll 'ave 'ee all sent away.'

'Oh do shut up! This is more important than your bloody hedges, Mr Bugger,' Nell called back at him.

'Listen girls,' said Pauline calmly, 'we'll meet outside Mr Knowles's house tonight and talk to him. Meanwhile, let's keep Mr Bugger quiet.'

At seven that evening we assembled in Egloshayle

road. Passers-by stopped and watched as we marched up to Mr Knowles's front door with Nell pushing her way to the fore.

'Leave 'im to me, girls. Me old man didn't throw pots and pans for nothin' an' I just might get 'im to talk. Yeah, watch me.'

She banged on the door knocker and instantly the dog started barking. The barking turned to growling when Mr Knowles began to open the door.

'What . . .?'

'Listen mate, you ain't sending our pals anywhere,' Nell said angrily. 'We're all in this bloody Land Army together!'

The little dog bared his teeth and Nell backed a few steps.

'Please, Mr Knowles, let us stay. We'll work hard and we'll never take another day off,' Bunny told him sweetly.

'It's too late, once too often you've . . .'

'We'll do anything if only you let us stay,' vowed Kay.

'Then go home and be ready for me in the morning.' With this Mr Knowles quickly shut the door in our faces.

Jackie turned. 'Nasty little man,' she hissed. 'The bastard.'

There seemed nothing else to do but retreat, blaming Bill Craddock for this unfortunate episode and hoping that the transfer of the three girls wasn't to be permanent.

Just before eight next morning I left Kay sitting on the bed with her kitbag packed and standing on the floor beside her. I was going to miss her but somehow I knew that it wouldn't be long before I saw her again. What I didn't realize was how soon it was to be!

Three days had passed since Kay, Jackie and Bunny had been taken to a hostel in St Erth, a village not so far from Penzance. We continued to clean the fields ready for ploughing. Day after day we sat in circles throwing the unwanted stones into a heap in the middle of the circles and the only consolation we got from this boring job was a glorious suntan! Arriving home on this third day I was surprised to be met by Kay; she stood at the front door looking jubilant.

'When did you get back?' I asked in astonishment.

'Soon after you went to work this morning,' she replied. 'We've run away from the hostel!' she added smiling.

'How did you get away?'

'We got up very early, threw our kitbags out of a window and then jumped out on to a slag heap and ran down the drive before anyone was awake. Then we caught a train to Bodmin.'

'I wonder what will happen when Mr Knowles finds out.'

'Don't worry,' she giggled, 'he knows. As usual he didn't say much. He simply told us to go back to work with you all tomorrow. We've promised to work hard in future.'

When we got to St Teath the following day and jumped from the lorry, Leonard spotted the returned three girls and stared in disbelief. 'So, you buggers are back again!' he smiled.

Chapter 14

The Petition

THE following two weeks dragged by slowly but we were into the month of June and our second leave was almost due. The fields that we had been working in were now full of mounds of stones that we had gathered and were waiting to be carried away by tractor to the nearest quarry. While we sat in circles, Leonard spent his time walking around the adjoining fields looking for signs of any weakness in the hedges. Every day we carried paper and pencils to work and when Leonard was far enough away from us we would write letters, either to parents or boyfriends. The social life was now almost non-existent. The nearest lads were the Fleet Air Arm based at St Merryn, nearly fifteen miles away, and the sailors would come by coach for the occasional dances that were held.

Mr Gill was exultant that he could now take his dog, Spot, for a walk in peace. In his own words to Mrs Gill: 'It's so peaceful without being pestered by the thundering noise of the thundering goddamned Yankee lorries all over the place, Sarah.'

'But, Father, they were nice boys and I do miss them.' This kind remark brought the inevitable 'Mmm!' accompanied by a triumphant twinkle in his eyes.

However, here we were on yet another beautiful day sitting in circles, becoming increasingly bored as the piles of stones grew higher. Every song we knew had been sung over and over again and now Bunny was resorting to telling our fortunes from the tea leaves left in the bottom of our flask cups! My turn came.

'You, Pat, I see on a farm. There is rather a short man, he is wearing a cap and is standing near some cows. You are not alone for I see two other girls alongside you,' Bunny informed me.

'Oh well,' I thought, and promptly laughed it off.

Kay drank the last of her tea and passed her cup to Bunny.

'That's funny,' said Bunny, scanning the cup, 'I can see a man almost identical to the one in Pat's cup.'

Jackie tipped her cup upside down and peered into the bottom. 'All I can see are bleedin' spuds, stones and mists. There's not a Yank in sight. When we've had our leave I'm resigning.'

'Let's not act in haste,' Pauline advised. 'After all, we've had some fun, haven't we?' Then she added wistfully, 'I must admit l would like to go back to Kent.'

'If we were put on private farms there would at least be more variety and—' I didn't get any farther for Jackie butted in.

'What?' she shouted, 'After being with that sodding carrot farmer – you must he mad!'

'They can't possibly all be like him,' I told her doubtfully.

Jackie looked at me disdainfully before turning to the other girls who had stopped work and gathered near: 'She's mad!'

'What about writing a petition complaining first and see what happens?' suggested Jimmy, 'It can't do any harm, let's try. Who's got a clean piece of paper?'

We all agreed and Phyllis produced a sheet of paper. After writing various complaints of backaches, head-aches and nosebleeds (all of which the local doctor would vouch for), we added BOREDOM in capital letters. The piece of paper was signed by each in turn and was consequently covered by dirty brown marks from our hands. This petition was done while Leonard was out of sight but on his return he looked puzzled. Rubbing his hand over his chin and with a frown on his face he asked, 'What are you buggers up to now?'

When told of our decision his hand fell from his chin but the frown remained as he spoke. 'Well! Do you think our lads abroad fighting have got it any easier? I s'pose I'll as likely get another lot of maids but you won't all be set free. Some of 'ee may be wanted to be rat catchers!' This last sentence he said with a broad grin and a great deal of satisfaction.

For the first time in nearly ten months we had no

THE PETITION

answer, we simply looked blankly into space. Rat catching? There had always been a bit of rivalry between the rat catchers and the girls who worked on the actual land. Nobody seemed to know why, unless it was the fact that our gang tumbled into a lorry each morning while they rode around in tidy small vans.

The silence was at last broken by a ghastly moan that came from Jackie. 'Rats? Rats?' she shuddered as she repeated the words, 'The bloody things can run wild. Ugh!' Lighting a cigarette she inhaled deeply, still shuddering at the thought. In spite of the heat of the day we all shivered at the prospect of harvesting rats – dead or alive.

Leonard was aware of our reaction and sat down on the earth beside us and spoke in a very quiet tone, unusual to him.

'Listen, you've got the sun tan you wanted. You've got the uniform you chose to wear. Now you must live up to the badge you were given or go back to the cities and face the bombs again. Think again girls' (the omission of 'buggers' went unheeded, but was significant), 'if you were in any other service you wouldn't have me taking your nonsense, you would be standing to attention and accused of mutiny!

'I'll tell 'ee something else, too. You've been a damned headache to me but I've enjoyed being with you. There's been no boredom for me trying to sort you lot out and getting some work out of 'ee. God

163

knows it's been plain 'ell at times. A mixed bunch you be but I've had many a chuckle. Take your leave but please come back.' He stood up and looked directly at Bunny and said, 'Wherever you go, maid, remember that small, brown box you carry is for your gas-mask and not the muck you put over your face.'

That evening we gathered in the Cornish Arms and discussed the possibility of being transferred into the Rat Catching department. We were not prepared to take the chance, we would resign or get a doctor's certificate! We dropped the petition into the red pillar box without a word to Mr Knowles.

A few days later we went home for our summer leave.

Chapter 15

Back to the Land

STANDING once again on the platform at Paddington station, I realized just how happy l was feeling about returning to the land. No, it was more than just the land, it was Cornwall. In spite of mists, muck and the moans of backaches, the county had a strong appeal for me. The rugged cliffs around Tintagel were beautiful, as were the small coves that we had discovered while having lunch breaks. The stark, bleak moors, of course, gave one a feeling of isolation when the mists settled around, but with the gang was it really as bad as we had made ourselves believe?

The small town of Wadebridge was attractive and had the added charm of the river Camel winding its way for miles, passing the house that belonged to Mr and Mrs Gill. Hadn't it been lovely to have had the freedom of borrowing Mr Gill's small boat to paddle up the river, to tramp through the woods that lay a few miles away? Apart from working hours there were no restrictions on our liberty.

Taking all this into consideration, weighing the pros and cons, then shouldn't we count our blessings during these unfortunate years of war? These were my thoughts as I stood waiting to board the train, at the same time keeping a look out for Kay. We had been living together like sisters for months and it would be sad to part. And as for Pauline, she had been a tower of strength in moments of crisis and had become a special friend.

Kay appeared and we got into a compartment but couldn't settle until we had walked the corridor of the train to see if all the gang had returned. They had, but from the chatter that took place between us during the journey back to the West, I suspected that there were several girls who were still undecided as to what to do. Before we disbanded at Wadebridge station it was arranged that we meet after church next day.

Sunday brought varied resolutions. Jackie was certain that nothing would overcome her dislike and fear of cows but as she put it, 'There might be Yanks somewhere near, so . . .' Kay wasn't averse to giving the Land Army another try, at least, for a while longer. We could only await the outcome of the petition now. It was to come the very next day!

Kay and I were about to leave the house for work when Mr Knowles walked up the pathway. Mrs Gill went to open the door and we followed her. The little man ignored Mrs Gill by looking over her shoulder at us, his face rather grave.

'Be outside the church in ten minutes. There's no work today but I want to talk to you all.' His voice sounded serious, too. Leaving our lunch boxes in the hall we glanced at Mr Gill who was peering out of the bay window, his cigarette and holder dangling from his mouth and his face full of bewilderment.

'What can the matter be, dears?' whispered Mrs Gill.

'We really don't know yet,' Kay answered.

'No, but we are about to find out very soon,' I said.

Unknown to us, this was to be the last time the gang members were to be together. We watched Mr Knowles slowly advance towards us, his little dog at his heels. What had he to tell us?

'Well, you've got what you wanted,' he began. 'Mr Wilson will be here from Truro this afternoon to take some of you to private farms; others will be sent back up country. Go back and pack your kitbags and wait.' He then warned us, again in a serious voice, 'Don't any of you leave your billets till he comes or you will be in trouble.'

Before we dispersed Jackie whispered to Kay, 'Wherever you go I want to go too.' These two had also become firm friends but would any friendship be taken into consideration now? In just a few hours we would know what Truro office had in store for us. When we told Mrs Gill the tears sprang to her eyes and she turned to her husband. 'Father, the girls are leaving us.'

167

'Mmm! Mmm! What be it for this time, Sarah?' he gloated.

'For good, they'll not be back. Oh! My dear life!' She ran into the kitchen, the tears now streaming down her face. Shortly after 3 o'clock a yellow van drew up and Mr Wilson came to the door. 'Come along you two, you're off to a place called Nancegollan and I need a third girl, yes, another girl.'

'Jackie!' cried Kay. 'Get my mate Jackie else we two don't go either!' Dare we still dictate what we wanted, where we would go?

Obviously Mr Wilson was now confused. However, within fifteen minutes the three of us were sitting in the van with this man, heading for an unknown place and we had no idea in which direction we were travelling! To add misery to the journey, Jackie kept moaning that she only had a few cigarettes and needed more.

'Couldn't you stop at a shop along the way, mate?' she wheedled.

'No time, no time!' replied an agitated Mr Wilson swerving to avoid a horse and cart laden with straw. Reaching a crossroads he swung the van around, swearing under his breath. 'I've lost my bloody way, girls. Keep quiet while I think, will you?'

We seemed to drive round in circles but finally stopped outside a row of small cottages where Jackie was told to get out.

'I'm not bloody well going to be on my own, am I?'

she wailed. 'I've got only one fag left. Christ! Where's the shop, mate?'

'I've no idea,' Mr Wilson replied sympathetically. 'It's past 5 o'clock. I haven't been to this place before but maybe there's a pub nearby where you'll be able to get some later.'

We watched Jackie walk dejectedly towards the cottage before driving a few yards on to where Kay and I were to be taken. Struggling with our kitbags we reached the brown door which was swung open by an elderly lady who immediately demanded that we take our shoes off before going upstairs.

'Tea has been ready these ages,' she grumbled, 'so make haste.'

In the small bedroom I faced Kay. 'I'm not unpacking because I'm not stopping here. How do you feel?'

'Like you, I don't know whether to laugh or cry, but Mr Wilson has gone so what do we do?'

'Find Jackie. I bet she won't be staying in her billet either!'

Telling the lady we were 'Sorry, but we're not hungry,' we made a quick exit and met Jackie running towards us. 'Sod this for a lark,' she shouted, 'I'm going to find the nearest station.'

Walking up the narrow road we came to crossroads. To the right was the village post office, to the left lay the means of escape – a railway station! With relief we approached the porter, only to be told that the last train to London had gone. What now? And what were we going to use for money? The allowance of 19/11d a week left little to be saved, and we relied on the free travelling-leave vouchers. There was another solution – I hoped!

'I'll ring the Agriculture Committee at Truro and tell them it's to be a farm or else!'

Ignoring Jackie's shudders I entered the telephone box feeling a mixture of temper and trepidation. There was nothing more to lose and we were not going to be shunted around like cattle!

When the receiver was picked up at Truro a male voice asked if he could help. 'Help?' I shouted into the phone. 'Of course you can help. You *must* help. Three of us are stranded in the middle of nowhere, there's not a soul in sight and where the devil are we supposed to work? I just thought I'd let you know that you have now lost three conscientious land girls.'

'Please don't leave,' the gentleman's voice begged. 'Someone will be with you in an hour so. Stay by the village post office.'

We went back to the cottages, picked up our kitbags and sat waiting, still listening to Jackie moaning about her last fag!

The same yellow van screeched to a halt an hour later. Mr Wilson put his head out of the van window. 'Jump in again,' he told us wearily, 'I'll find a farm for you somewhere before it gets dark. Someone may need three stupid and rebellious girls but, by God, I'll feel sorry for the farmer, though!'

Fifteen minutes later we were going down a drive lined with trees. A large stone farmhouse came into view just above a farmyard. Mr Wilson drew to a halt, wiped the sweat from his brow and walked up a short pathway to the farmhouse door and knocked. A few minutes later a young woman followed him back to the van.

She looked into the van at us and her first words came as a shock. 'Can you milk cows?' she asked.

'Oh! No!' I felt the tight pressure of Jackie's hand on my arm. 'Have you ever planted cabbage?' was the next question.

'No, but we'll try,' Kay and I said together.

'All right, I'll take them on a month's trial,' said the woman and with a sigh of relief Mr Wilson drove away.

We were shown into a large kitchen and there sat the farmer in an armchair. He wasn't very tall and a cap was pushed to the back of his head. So, Bunny was right in her fortune telling! We fell into a large double bed that night, realizing that this was the third house we had been billeted in that day!

Chapter 16

Nature Takes its Course

'HELL's bloody bells!' The words came slowly and sleepily from Jackie as we were aroused by tapping on the bedroom door.

'It's 7 o'clock, girls. Breakfast and work in half an hour.' The door opened slightly and the woman added, 'Don't make a noise for I've two young children still sleeping.'

While dressing I glanced out of the window that overlooked the farmyard and saw a herd of cows standing still, disregarding the movements of two young men who were weaving their way between them. It was obviously the morning milking time.

'Come and watch this, you two,' I said, pulling on my jumper. 'There's surely nothing to be afraid of. No shouts, no screams.'

'Ugh!' Disdain was written on Jackie's face, 'Oh Christ, I'll never go near them.' Goose pimples rose on her arms.

'Stop worrying and hurry, we've to find the bathroom,'

Kay said with impatience. 'You never stop moaning, do you?'

There were four more doors leading from the landing and we opened each one cautiously as we looked for the bathroom. Two little girls occupied one of the rooms and the others were also bedrooms.

'Where the hell do we wash?' asked Jackie.

The farmer's wife had heard us and quickly informed us that there were bowls and water downstairs in the back kitchen!

Drying our faces on a roller towel hanging from a wall, Jackie spoke her disapproval in one word. 'Peasants!' she hissed. I wondered. A lovely house but why no bathroom?

We had barely finished breakfast when the farmer appeared.

'Cummus on, cummus on. The tractor and men are waiting and the day isn't that long,' he said, taking a cigarette from his pocket and lighting it.

'Fags!' cried Jackie. 'Oh mister, I ain't had one for hours. Do me a favour, I'm dying for one.'

With a twinkle in his blue eyes he handed her the packet: 'Don't make a habit of it, they are hard to come by.'

Following our new boss we were relieved to turn right towards the tractor instead of left where the dreaded cows were still standing, almost stationary, in the yard. The two young men I had seen earlier sat on the trailer with an elderly man alongside. Obeying the next order we jumped up on the vehicle and sat amongst boxes of cabbages. Not a word was spoken during the short journey to a nearby field, the men just eyeing us, obviously wondering where we had suddenly sprung from! Reaching the field, the trailer was unloaded and a bundle of plants was thrust into our arms. We were each told to work alongside one of the men.

'They are the "shovellers" and you girls are the "stickers", with any brains you should get the hang of it,' the farmer stated, again with a twinkle in his eyes.

The earth had been ploughed, rolled and marked in rows so as to guide the required straightness.

'May as well know who we're working with. What you called?' asked the elderly man. We introduced ourselves and learned that he answered to the name of 'Uncle Walter'. He nodded towards the other two, 'They be brothers, William and Leonard.'

'What's he called?' Jackie asked William with a side look at the farmer who was repeating the words, 'Cummus on.'

'He's Joe. Joe Pascoe.'

'Is he a slave driver?'

William smiled, 'You'll soon find out for yourself!'

I found myself at the side of the self-appointed Uncle. With one foot, he heeled the spade into the ground and slightly turned it so that I would be able insert the young plant. When he withdrew the spade the earth would fall back to keep the plant in its place. But when I bent down and reached across my body to lay the first plant I dropped the remaining armful to the ground.

'Huh! land girls! We've 'ad 'em 'ere before and they've not much mind to work. Use your other arm, maid,' growled Uncle Walter, 'Be easier for me.'

'I'm left-handed so I can't. You use your other foot,' I said.

Spitting on his hands before transferring the shovel to his left side, he muttered , 'And now me other boot'll go through!'

Two hours later we sat by the hedge and Jackie was puffing on a Woodbine that she had cadged from Leonard. With our feet extended in front of us we couldn't fail to notice that all three men had slits and holes in just one of their boots.

'You poor sods,' Jackie commiserated, 'it's hard work and not much bleedin' money. Why do you do it?'

'Oh, these holes are caused by the shovel during the planting season,' said William without a trace of self-pity. 'Sometimes we wear a pair of boots out in a week!'

'I *knew* it! He's another bloody slave driver. I'm not staying a month, he can stick his own plants.'

Kay looked to the far end of the field, 'And look at that poor sod over there, he hasn't stopped walking all morning.' Our eyes followed hers and we watched a man driving a horse up and down with no thought of stopping, let alone moaning.

'That's Jimmy. He bears blisters on his feet and 'tween his toes. Only time he rides is when he takes the horse to the blacksmith, so what you wailin' for?' Uncle Walter scoffed. He seemed to take a delight in seeing Jackie's doleful expression and carried on. 'Take it from me, tis 'ard work, maid. Wait till we bring the corn in, you'll be in the fields till dark. I'm a widow-man and it's a wisht life sometimes. Then there's the milking . . .' With great satisfaction he struck a match, put it to the bowl of his pipe and blew some quick blasts of smoke into the air. 'And another thing, maid, there's no Yanks round this 'ere part of the world.'

'Gawd! No Yanks, no fags . . .' Jackie didn't finish because Kay butted in. 'And there's no bathroom, how does a body . . .?'

'That's what them twos are called,' intercepted Uncle Walter, pointing to William and his brother who were working alongside us.

'Body? B.O.D.Y.?' I asked, turning to William and Leonard who were quickly rising from the ground.

'Yes,' said William grabbing his shovel, 'that's their family name but right now it stands for Bend Over Darlin' Yeu! cos here comes Joe, backs down!'

Two days later, Kay, Jackie and I were standing by the tractor waiting for the men to finish in the yard when Joe hurried towards us from the mowhay. 'Go into the barn and sweep the floor until we're ready for you,' he said and quickly walked to the yard.

There were several small dusty windows overlooking the yard and we peered through one of them. A bull was being led towards a small cow while the other four men stood at various points.

'Hold the heifer still. Dammit, hold the heifer still!'

Being unfamiliar with bovine periods of development the word reached our ears like 'effer', someone must indeed, be angry!

'So! They swear like troopers too,' Jackie said with incredulity. Now in future I'll let it rip!'

Continuing to gaze from the window, we saw the bull led to the cow and mount her. Only at that moment did we realize why we had been sent to the barn! This wasn't meant for our eyes!

'Oh God! That poor bleedin' cow, that does it!' Jackie's face had turned pale. Kay and I simply burst out laughing at her reaction and our own naivety!

At the end of the third week Kay and Jackie packed their kitbags and returned to London. Saying farewell to them at the station wasn't easy but we promised to keep in touch. I walked back to the farm thinking of Jackie's last words to me: 'Keep your bloody farms, cows, bulls and heifers and do his dirty work. I'm off and away at last, thank God!'

I didn't feel at all discouraged at being left alone but I did wonder how long it would be before I too returned to urban life. The only certainty was that the 'gang' had now well and truly broken up and the war had been on for almost five years.

Chapter 17

The Last Day

A WEEK had passed since I had been left 'on my own' and I continued to hover around the cowshed watching the men and the local land girl, Frances, do the early morning milking. The nearest I had got to the cows was in front of them to feed them and a concrete wall divided us! My contribution towards producing dairy products amounted to throwing the allotted quantity of hay into the cow troughs and beating a hasty retreat! Now the words I expected and dreaded reached my ears; I felt my stomach perform a somersault and inwardly I panicked.

'It's about time you put your hand to milking, Pat. The lorry collecting the churns is coming earlier and earlier and all you're doing is fooching around watching we,' said Joe. 'Cummus on and make a start.'

'Please give me a quiet cow,' I begged, 'and stay near me.'

I picked up a three-legged stool and empty pail and stepped between two cows. Gripping the pail tightly between my knees I sat on the stool at the rear end of a roan cow and looked at the pendulous bag that awaited my attention.

'Get your hands round two teats, pull and squeeze. No dammit! Not one from the front and one from the back, the two in front!' Joe's agitation only made me feel even more panicky. The cow changed position. 'She's moving!' I cried.

'So should you be. 'Old 'ard and shove your 'ead in the flank.'

'The flank? Where's that?'

'Cummus on, else she'll start stanking and 'old 'er milk.'

My head was pushed firmly between the cow's ribs and hip.

'Oh Jackie,' I thought, 'how wise you were, how foolish I am!'

Minutes later a trickle of white liquid oozed from one of the teats, it ran to my wrist and then down my arm.

'Milk! I've got some!' my voice echoed into the pail.

'What the 'ell did you expect, gin and orange?' laughed Joe.

Inspired by this remark that implied I was an idiot I gained courage and relaxed. Very slowly (and maybe painfully for the cow) the milk fell in odd drops and squirts. My vision had come true! Now I felt like a *real* land girl, now I could boast! Oblivious of time, I sat hunched, pulling and squeezing. The feeling of achievement was quickly shattered when I heard several impatient tuts coming from Joe.

'Get up, maid, get up, do. You're doing more 'arm than good now and she's got to be stripped yet. Walter! Come 'ere and finish 'er.'

'Stripping', I knew, meant returning to the cows to squeeze the last drop of milk from the udders.

Easing myself up I was reminded in no uncertain terms that I hadn't all the space I wanted. A large brown body pushed into my back, I was sandwiched between two cows and rigid with terror.

'Don't be 'urried,' Joe laughed, pushing the cows apart. I quickly glanced at Uncle Walter as he shuffled to a halt near the stall. Through a cloud of smoke an unmistakable expression of gloating spread across his face. Taking the pipe from his mouth he said gleefully, 'Wait till you face the bull, maid!'

This man irritated me. Each morning when Frances arrived, he would order her with assumed authority, 'Frances, give the bull some hay.' Frances would meekly obey. Just let him command me to feed the mate of this herd because he himself was faint-hearted! As it was, I stepped meekly away with stool and pail!

Autumn. Depending on the weather, two crops filled the days. When it was dry and sunny, corn took priority over broccoli planting, which we had started as soon as the cabbage had finished. I enjoyed every moment of 'shocking', despite the scratches on my arms caused by handling the sheaves of corn. The fields of grain took on a lovely pattern of golden stooks which we left in the fields for a few more days to dry out before carrying them into the mowhay for building into stacks. When we came to the end of harvesting, it was customary for all farm hands to ride in with the last load of corn. As the wagon filled and grew higher with the remaining sheaves, Joe appeared carrying an enamel jug and cups. It was dusk so why this sudden consideration for our thirsts?

'Throw the last bit up and drink this,' Joe said pleasantly.

I took a cup and as he poured I sniffed the acrid smell. 'This isn't tea, it smells like beer. Is it?'

'Iss. Herbie beer. Good 'ome brew!' Joe's eyes sparkled.

I slowly sipped the liquid and my head began to reel. Uncle Walter gulped down his cupful and asked for another. I watched him swallow the second cupful and smack his lips together. ''Tis good stuff, Joe,' he slurred.

'Another, Walter?' Joe offered with a fiendish smile.

Still sipping my first drink I watched Uncle Walter raise his arm and cup for the third time and swallow the good 'ome brew. 'Cummus on now, get up on the load,' said Joe.

With a pull from William on top and a push from Jimmy, I landed in a heap and clutched a rope. Getting on my knees I saw Uncle Walter staggering towards the hedge. 'What's the matter with him?' I asked, suspecting the beer.

'Oh, that's usual for him, he dearly likes the drink,' answered Jimmy, laughing. 'He'll end up in the hedge singing, sure 'nough.'

It was now my turn to gloat!

'Serves him right,' I expressed with pleasure, 'perhaps that lot will keep him silent for a few days!'

It didn't! As we moved off in the wagon, Uncle Walter raised his voice in song. From one bar of 'Drink to me Only' he switched to a hymn and burst out, 'All is safely gathered in . . .'

I was duly issued with a bicycle and this enabled me to ride to various villages and the small social institute at Nancegollan. My only complaint now was the lack of a bathroom.

'As soon as the war is over and the men come home we'll have one,' explained Mrs Pascoe, 'until then we have to carry on washing in the back kitchen. And while I'm on the subject of water,' she went on, 'we are soon to have a tuberculosis test so in future you will have to scrub the cowshed walls clean after milking every morning!'

I opened my mouth to argue about this and promptly

closed it again, knowing that cleanliness was absolutely essential for this vital test. I spent many hours scrubbing the dried dung from the walls and the reward for this arduous task was to hear from the Milk Marketing Board that it was the cleanest cowshed for miles!

I graduated from the cowshed to the piggery and dung-spreading! Faith was put in my ability to 'bring the cows in', feed the chickens and 'bus' the calves. Uncle Walter continued to annoy Frances and me by deliberately cleaning his pipe in the dairy right after we had cleaned it. Any comment from me went unheeded: he simply growled, 'You're teasy, maid, teasy as an adder,' and purposely puffed his pipe with more vigour, leaving us standing in a cloud of smoke while he went, he said, to 'make tracks 'ome and get some tea.'

Christmas came and I sat in the train heading to London for my third leave. Looking up at the luggage rack I recalled how Nell had taken her 'bleedin' live chicken' home the previous year and caused so much laughter. Now here was I, travelling with the same kind of bird but there was a difference. Mine was dead, plucked, cleaned and ready for the oven!

I had no qualms about returning to Cornwall after my leave. We entered a new year and the world had entered its sixth year of war. Back on the farm it was difficult to realize that so much conflict was going on. The only constant reminder seemed to be clothing coupons and Uncle Walter's snide remarks, telling me I was 'opeless and piskey-led and the sooner I went back upalong the better! I assumed this was because I ignored any orders he chose to give me until I had double-checked!

Throughout winter and into spring, odd days of 'threshing' took place. Men were borrowed from nearby farms and also lent for this occasion. I detested the whole business, for although land girls were given the supposedly easiest job of carrying dust into the barn, it was also the dirtiest!

It was now old man Pascoe's turn to borrow labour and I was sent to help. I cycled slowly to his farm deliberately wasting time. Here, indeed, was a slave driver who brought a chair out to the fields to sit and watch proceedings, and no slacking!

Jumping from my bicycle, I was met by the old man who sat on a stool giving his whole attention to what was going on around – nothing was going to miss his inspection! Scowling at me he raised a stick. 'Girl,' he said gruffly, 'pick up a crail and work.'

The very thought of being spoken to in this nameless way antagonized me. Pretending not to hear or see him, I looked to the top of the rick where Joe was busy pitching sheaves. He looked back. There was no sympathy from him so I picked up a crail and began filling it with dust. Once filled, I lugged it on my back and took it across the yard, emptied the lot onto a growing pile and slowly walked back to the threshing machine for more. An hour or so went by and then a sharp wind whipped through the shed where the machine was chugging away. My hair became a tangled mess and in no time my eyes were smarting from the minute particles of barley that were blowing everywhere. Emptying yet another crail I made for the barn where William was tipping sacks of corn onto the floor. By now I could hardly see. I took my handkerchief from my pocket, shook the dust from it and handed it to William. While he tried to extract the dust and dirt from my eyes, old man Pascoe's voice bellowed across the yard. 'Maid, what you about? The dust is building up so come out of the barn!'

'Who does he bloody well think he's talking to?' I asked William.

'Gesson, don't worry. If I were you I'd go home,' said William. Yes! That's what I'd do right now! With my temper rising and eyes burning, I walked to my bicycle propped against the wall and waited for the bellowing to start again.

'Dammit girl! Come back and do as I say, dammit!' From the corner of my eye I saw the old man trying to rise from his stool with the aid of a stick but I ignored him. I looked at no one. Wheeling my bike away from the horrid mess of threshing I swore I would never work for the grumpy old man again. On my way back to the farm I took the cows in from the field for evening milking, an act to cover up for my deserting the nasty task of threshing. To my surprise, not a word was said by Joe!

Among the activities of Lower Pengwedna farm was a 'Field Day'. Farmers, young and old, brought an assortment of bullocks and horses to be judged, and a ploughing match followed. When the competitions ended, Frances and I got on with the milking. We had almost finished washing the cowshed when in walked a group of young farmers offering their assistance. Not wishing to be hindered, we promptly told them to 'clear off'. An argument followed, tempers rose and in no time at all we were throwing buckets of water at each other! The outcome of this juvenile saturation was a 'date' to go to a dance in Helston that night!

The 8th of May dawned. Unaware that history was being made we carried on working normally until just before mid-day when I saw Joan, the land girl working on a neighbouring farm, frantically cycling down the drive.

'Pat,' she burst out, 'the war is over!'

I ran into the farmhouse and told Mrs Pascoe.

'Don't joke, Pat. There are many lads from this area away fighting, some even reported missing. A rumour like that isn't clever.'

'But it's not a rumour and I'm not joking. Turn on the radio.'

We heard the peal of bells and a jubilant voice

broadcasting that it was officially VE Day. Alas, the Japanese hadn't surrendered, but hopefully, it wouldn't be long before they did. 'Call in tonight, Joan,' Joe told her, 'and we'll celebrate.'

A few mixed drinks that night and I was no longer sober. I fell on my bed feeling sick and wishing I was dead!

During the following weeks many villages celebrated and held carnivals. Along with two other land girls, Frances and I found ourselves caught up in the gaiety of entering one. Joe had no hesitation in lending us one of his horses and a trailer. The trailer was scrubbed clean and Jimmy spent hours grooming the horse and polishing the decorative brasses in his spare time. Such was the devotion of a good horseman.

Off we set, happy and confident that our slogan of 'Intense Cultivation' would be a winner! We came close, with only the worthy and patriotic float 'Britannia' beating us.

A few days after this event I became engaged to the young farmer who had taken me to the dance in Helston, but I continued to stay in the WLA until the following May when I sent in my resignation, for I needed time to return to London and prepare for my wedding.

Truro asked me to return my uniform and bicycle, in exchange for which I would receive some clothing coupons. I needed the coupons badly to allow me to buy my wedding dress and other new clothes.

When I was packing my kitbag, a feeling of emptiness assailed me. I reached in and pulled out my wellingtons. No! I wouldn't return these. After all, hadn't they played a large part in preparing me to be a farmer's wife?

Women's
Land Army

Women's
Timber Corps

*The Government wishes to express to
you its profound gratitude for your
unsparing efforts as a loyal and devoted
member of the Women's Land Army/
Women's Timber Corps at a time when our country
depended upon you for its survival.*

Gordon Brown

July
2008

Rt Hon Gordon Brown MP
Prime Minister

Other Books from Old Pond Publishing

Charismatic Cows and Beefcake Bulls

Sonia Kurta's memories of farm work as a young girl are mostly set in Cornwall on the great Caerhays estate. She joined the Land Army in 1943 and stayed until it was disbanded in 1950. Paperback

Farmer's Boy

Michael Hawker's detailed recollections of work on north Devon farms in the 1940s and 1950s. Paperback.

Land Girls at the Old Rectory

An entertaining account by Irene Grimwood of what it was like for a town girl to join the Land Army in 1939-45. She and her lively friends learned to hoe, build stacks and cope with livestock as well as American servicemen. Paperback.

A Land Girl's War

Joan Snelling became a tractor driver during her wartime service in Norfolk. Her book recalls the dangers and tragedies of the period as well as its lighter side and her romance with an RAF pilot. Paperback.

In a Long Day   DAVID KINDRED AND ROGER SMITH

Two hundred captioned photographs of farm work and village life in Suffolk 1925–33. Paperback.

The Rural World of Eric Guy   JONATHAN BROWN

From the 1930s to the 1960s Eric Guy photographed the downland scene around his Berkshire base. Jonathan Brown has selected 174 of his most striking photographs and provides a knowledgeable text. Paperback

The Traditional Farming Year   PAUL HEINEY

Using many photographs from the archives of *Farmer and Stockbreeder* magazine, Paul Heiney brings to life an agricultural year before the tractor and combine. Hardback.

Free complete catalogue:

Old Pond Publishing Ltd
Dencora Business Centre
36 White House Road, Ipswich IP1 5LT, United Kingdom
Secure online ordering: **www.oldpond.com**
Phone: 01473 238200   Fax: 01473 238201

About the Author

Pat was born in London. She left school at Dulwich just as war was declared in 1939. She immediately went to work in a factory as a machinist making greatcoats for the army.

When she was seventeen she volunteered for the Women's Land Army, inspired by the outdoor life and the uniform!

After the war, in 1946 she married a Cornish farmer's son, Gordon, and shared living in Polwin Manor farm with Gordon's brother and sister-in-law.

The farm building was very old and when there was heavy rain the water came in through the back door and flowed out through the front, leaving a trail of mud on the carpets. Both wives had babies whose health in this building was a cause for concern, so after three years the farm was sold.

Gordon took a manager's job at Gurlyn farm, Pat having made sure that the water works were in order. They had a second son and continued to have amusing ups and downs: a raging bull in the front garden and goats chewing washing from the line – but that's another story!

Kay, Pauline and Pat kept in close contact for over sixty years until, sadly, Kay and Pauline died.